TOUCHING GOD

TOUCHING GOD

A Book About
Children's Liturgies

Rev. W. Thomas Faucher

and

Ione C. Nieland

AVE MARIA PRESS
Notre Dame, Indiana 46556

Nihil Obstat and   John F. Donoghue
Imprimi Potest: Censor Librorum

Imprimatur: Sylvester W. Treinen, D.D.
   Bishop of Boise

Library of Congress Catalog Card No. 74-26313
International Standard Book Number: 0-87793-085-6
Photography: *Mark Holden* and *Fr. Joseph Muha*
Manufactured in the United States of America

In deep love,
this book is dedicated to the memory of
Msgr. John J. Creegan
1904-1974

CONTENTS

PREFACE

We offer this book as part of the growing literature on children's liturgy. If because of it one child somewhere is able to come closer to God, we have been completely successful.

We take as a principle that deep inside each man is a need to celebrate, to worship. From the very beginning of our lives, this need is present, and our initial experiences in fulfilling this need will determine much of our future ability to celebrate and to relate to God.

If those experiences are good ones, man will grow up being able to express himself in liturgy, to express himself in dialogue with God, to touch God. Thus we have the reason for what have come to be called "children's liturgies." (It is a bit frightening to think that, although Jesus tells us all to be children, we need to invent a term to describe the prayer of children that makes it different from our prayer.)

In addition to whatever academic training either of us brings to this book, we claim as our only real qualification that we have tried to celebrate Jesus with children. As a priest in a parish, and a lay teacher in a Catholic grade school, we have learned most of the things in this book by experience. We offer our conclusions as part of the constantly growing thinking of the Church.

Deep gratitude is due to many people who have made this book possible. First and foremost, to the children of St. Anthony's Parish, Pocatello, Idaho, and the children of Sacred Heart Parish, Boise. The book would not have been possible without the aid and support of the Liturgy Commission of the Diocese of Boise, and especially the chairman, Father Jerry Horton, and the Idaho Catholic Education Office. Special thanks should be given to Sister Laureen Marie Wright, O.S.B., who worked on some of the model liturgies, and to Mark Holden, Fr. Joseph Muha, Mr. Fred Cuoio, and the photo staff of Bishop Kelly High School for the pictures used throughout the book. Thanks are also due to the dedicated people who typed large sections of the manuscript, especially Mrs. Mary Johnson and Mrs. Mary Allen, and those whose constructive criticism helped edit and improve our work. Most of all we thank Bishop Sylvester Treinen of Boise, who encourages everyone to try.

Chapter 1

WHAT ARE CHILDREN'S LITURGIES?

For many of us, Mass is something that we adults (priests and laity) are used to, we have "done" it for many years. While we may have enjoyed the changes in the Church for the past few years, we still see Mass as something which is essentially an adult action which represents (depending on our theological orientation) only a sacrifice, or only a meal, or only a prayer, or only a duty, or at least something other than a celebration. A celebration contains all these aspects and many more. All too often adults believe children should be in church on Sunday because they "might as well learn young" just what is demanded of a Catholic.

Children's liturgy represents a different kind of thinking. It is a gathering of children to celebrate Jesus Christ on the level of the child, authentically part of the Church, but not the adult Church. If Jesus meant his Church to be truly the call to salvation for all men, then he also intended it for children, and not just for children as a stage for adulthood, but children as they are.

But what is this children's liturgy? On the most elemental level, children's liturgy is a celebration in which the rites and symbols of the Church are simplified and made intimate. Most of all, it is bringing children to Jesus, and letting them get to know one another.

Gabe Huck expresses it well in the *Liturgy Committee Handbook,* when he says:

> When we speak of a children's liturgy we mean something where children feel utterly free to be themselves . . . a celebration which springs from the good news of Jesus.

That approach rules out from the start any hint of gimmickry to "keep the kids from being bored" at a basically adult liturgy. It demands ritual, difficult as this may be when the home life is lacking any ritual with a religious content. But the kinds of ritual chosen and the approach to them are determined by the demand to *take the children as they are.*

Children know what the word "celebration" means and they should be able to find just that when they come to a liturgy. There is a very simple criterion for evaluating children's liturgies: we need only observe the children. If it isn't coming through that there is good news for them here, at this time and place, then the liturgy has fallen short.[1]

The debate of recent years on the subject of children's liturgies has taken the form of two sides: those who advocate them and those who do not. The latter group divides into those who feel children should attend an adult church, and those who feel that the Eucharistic liturgy is not capable of being made intimate for children and new paraliturgical rites should be created. The poorly done "extremes" in so-called children's liturgies in various places have strengthened the positions of those who oppose them.

But true children's liturgies can and are being celebrated: liturgies which are ritual activity utterly in keeping with the ways of children and the nature of the Church's mysteries. These liturgies are not adult liturgy simplified or stripped down to be understandable by children. On the contrary, they are the mystery of worship—touching God—celebrated authentically by children. There is a fundamental principle which must be grasped: Children's liturgies are built by using the manner in which the children live, emote, relate, etc.; they are not simplified adult liturgies.

As part of an understanding of children's liturgy, we need to understand that liturgy always takes place in a context, an atmosphere. Atmosphere in liturgy is created by many things. It is more than just the room or the music or the colors or any of those things. It is a very subtle and yet real dialogue between good and evil, the seen and the unseen, the here and beyond, between self and God, between priest and people. In liturgy, all of us, adults and children must be raised to a point of tension and paradox before we can truly see just what it is that we are doing. Liturgy is "touching God" and touching God is not easy.

The "things" of liturgy are truly important—music, color, mood—not in themselves but as means to the end. We are people who are deeply affected by the setting we are in, what we are like at any moment. In a group context, that setting can affect our entire relationship with that group and its actions.

---

1. *Liturgy Committee Handbook: A Nine-Week Study Guide,* The LIturgical Conference, Washington, D.C.

The list of elements which are used to build children's liturgies is endless. We have selected just a few, to give some examples of what they are. Most of these elements also apply to adult liturgies.

ELEMENTS

Symbols have always been essential to rites of worship and to the transmission of the message of Jesus. But in a children's liturgy, the symbols of children are used, not the symbols of adults. Children live in a practical, touchable world, they are aware of the beauty and wonder of water, fire, rocks, plants, animals. It is through the use of these symbols, which are part of their world, that the worship of God and the message of Jesus can be best celebrated.

The *atmosphere* of children is one of wonder and excitement, of learning and curiosity and feeling and touching, seeing, laughing, crying. It is a difficult atmosphere for many adults. When that atmosphere is found in church it is especially difficult for some priests who have been trained to see reverence and correct church manners associated with quiet, docility. In the Church, since Vatican II, that type of atmosphere has become increasingly less important for children. It takes only a short time for children to be completely comfortable celebrating a liturgy on their level, sharing their wonder and excitement; it often takes a bit longer for adults to be as comfortable. Once that atmosphere is created, it is easily maintained. Children show a deep reverence, *in their own style,* of what the Church is.

A third element of a children's liturgy is the *adaptation of some parts of the Mass* into children's style. On an average day the atmosphere created for that liturgy would emphasize one or more aspects of the Mass, but probably not all. Some of the liturgies contained in this book are complete children's liturgies. But there are many more where only the readings or responses or thanksgiving or some other part has been worked out with the children, and the remaining parts of the liturgy retained from the Mass of the day. In the latter, the celebrant by his style and manner makes those aspects of the liturgy understandable to the children.

Oddly enough *tension* is an element of liturgy. Tension between sinful isolation and graced community. We can drift through life, not facing up to who we are. But Jesus Christ taught us, and demands of us, that we freely admit that we are not alone, that we cannot live alone. We are made to need God and to need the people of God. When we come forward to touch God in liturgy, we are exposing an ever-present temptation within ourselves. Throughout the liturgy, not just in the penitential rites, we can, on the one hand, remain uncommitted, alone, selfish by isolating ourselves or by escaping into unthinking mimicry of what those around us are doing. On the other hand, we can get personally involved, truly conscious of what our words and actions mean, even if that is something those around us are not doing. This is the tension of liturgy—whether or not to risk being aware of what an awesome thing it is we are doing.

Where this tension is lacking, either in adult or children's liturgies, liturgical atmosphere is lacking, and while bread and wine will become the body and blood of Jesus, it will bear a faint resemblance to the Last Supper where Jesus confronted Judas, where John and Peter debated the betrayal, where Jesus reported the coming denial, and contemplated the death he was to endure. Tension and uncertainty are essential, for it is the task of the entire celebration to overcome that uncertainty and tension for at least one moment in a common experience of God's relationship with man.

Music plays a large role in atmosphere, for man responds to music from a primordial need inside himself. Liturgy is call and response in all directions, a dialogue, trialogue, whatever—it is God and man and man and God talking, sometimes plain talk, and sometimes the deeper and more revealing talk of music and poetry. Music must be good and realistic, to express this dialogue, to carry revelation from God to man, from man to his fellowman, from man back to God.

Music establishes much of the atmosphere of any celebration; and its absence, unless specifically called for, is usually an indication that there is no liturgical atmosphere desired. Music forces man to respond either into community or into deeper isolation. That is why there is little room for poor music, for poor music sets a cheap and shoddy atmosphere, unless the music, while musically poor, is rich in emotional or psychological content for the worshiping people. Children appreciate this power of music more than adults do.

If liturgy is seen as only something to be done, according to frozen recipes, then to speak of *dynamism* is ridiculous. But liturgy is not a memorial play. Roman Catholic liturgical celebration of the Eucharist is an event which each time is the true reliving of the death and resurrection of Christ. It is alive and happening, limited in its power only by the faith of the community worshiping. The call to make it as close as possible to Holy Thursday, Good Friday, and Easter can be answered only gradually, as the community grows slowly in its own dynamic history. If the dynamic, unique element of a liturgy cannot be felt and understood, the atmosphere again is the poorer for it.

Lastly, all liturgy is related to *religious education* and the mystery of unfolding revelation. In children's liturgy, this is especially true. There should be a close relationship with the total lives of the children and what they do at home and in school, so that they truly have something to celebrate, and know what it means to bring their home life to share with Jesus and with one another. All liturgy is celebration of life, and if children can learn to celebrate each day, then maybe adults can too.

These are sketchy thoughts on children's liturgy. While there should be great effort to create good atmosphere at all liturgies, in those with children the need is even more critical because of the simplicity and openness of those celebrating children. Their initial attempts to touch God must be as wonderful as possible.

Chapter 2

HOW TO SET UP A CHILDREN'S LITURGY PROGRAM

It is a difficult thing actually to begin the whole process of having children's liturgies in a parish. But it can be done, and this section is only one possible way to go about it.

First of all, get all those involved together, explain and discuss what children's liturgy is, and pray about the idea. Depending on the parish, there will be some opposition, some real enthusiasm, and probably a great deal of apathy. That is all right, for a good children's liturgy program comes only in time. One thing to remember is the need for a shared vision on the part of all the adults involved, a vision achieved only by prayer and discussion. One of the major items to discuss and stress is that the one who is to plan the liturgy must truly be a part of the community he or she is working with. He must feel with and for the other members; he must understand and empathize with their needs; he must accept them and love them as they are; he must be one with them.

Secondly, explain what a "liturgy outline" is. A liturgy outline is a written form which, when filled out, guides the program of the Mass each day; it is the practical program of a children's liturgy. It can be well compared to the musical lines you need to write notes on when composing music, or the canvas needed to paint. One type of liturgy outline is found on pages 18-19. A liturgy outline should be filled out for each Mass, with a copy for the celebrant, a copy for the person in charge (the leader), and a copy for anyone else who will need one. Only when all those who will be planning liturgies are comfortable with the liturgy form will they be comfortable planning liturgies.

Third, set up some type of schedule of liturgies. In a parish with a school, there is usually a ready-made system. One or two classes can come to Mass each weekday on a regular basis, with perhaps the whole school or at least some larger section of it coming together on one day. In a CCD system, some type of schedule can be drawn up.

LITURGY FORM

Date: .... TIME: .... GROUP: ....

Theme: ....

....

Basic Symbols: ....

*Entrance Song: ....

Introduction: ....

Penitential Rite: ....

Prayer: .... Read from: ....

First Reading: .... Read from: ....

   Read by: ....

Response: .... Read from: ....

   Read by: ....

Second Reading: .... Read from: ....

   Read by: ....

*Gospel Acclamation: From: .... Sung: .... Tune: ....

   Or recited: .... Led by: ....

Gospel: .... Read from: ....

Homily: ....

Prayer of the Faithful: ....

Offering of Gifts: ....

   Carried by: ....

Offering Song: ....

Prayer over Gifts: .... Read from: ....

Eucharistic Prayer:

   Preface: ....

   *Holy, Holy, Holy: Recited: .... Sung: .... Tune: ....

   Prayer: Number: ....

   *Eucharistic Acclamation: Number .... Recited: .... Sung:..........

        E.A. Tune: ....

Doxology: Recited: .... Sung: .... Tune: ....

*Amen: Recited: .... Sung: .... Tune:...................

Our Father: Recited: .... Sung: .... Tune: ....

Rite of Peace: ....

Lamb of God: Recited: .... Sung: .... Tune: ....

Communion Form: ....

*Communion Song: ....

Thanksgiving: ....

....

Prayer: .... Read from: ....

Blessing: ....

Recessional Song: ....

N.B. * = should normally be sung

_____

General Instructions and Comments: ....

....

....

....

....

....

....

....

....

Additional readings or prayers: ....

....

....

....

....

....

....

Fourth, the priest must begin his own special preparation.

STEPS TO BE FOLLOWED

1) The teacher or leader considers what the class will be taking in religion classes during the coming weeks. A theme is chosen from the general point of the coming lessons. Next, the teacher goes to the *Ordo* and checks what the Church universal requires for the day in question. With the new regulations (Cf. *Directory for Masses with Children* #41 F) there is ample freedom for finding a reading that can be used. After the *Ordo* has been consulted, go to the lectionary and read the recommended readings for the day. If they fit the theme well, use them. If they do not, have someone in the class (if the group is old enough) find readings that do fit. If the group is not old enough, the planner must do it himself.

The planner should next focus on a specific need or interest of the community or concept to be taught. He should think of his concern in the light of the gospel and pray to understand it. It is important to remember that what the liturgy should celebrate is the good news of Jesus Christ, the Word of God.

2) Once the theme and readings are chosen, the rest of the liturgy falls into place quite well. Decide which parts of the Mass should be especially amplified to express the theme and to involve the children. There can be no rules about this for it changes from day to day, from class to class, depending on many different circumstances.

3) The planner could choose a selection from children's literature or educational materials such as a poem, parable, play, story, puppet show, or film that will enhance, enlarge and portray effectively the theme and message. This selection, perhaps "secular" in nature, is an existential presentation of scripture and should be used where it fits in best: after a short first reading from scripture, as a thanksgiving after Communion, in connection with the penitential rite, etc. In a children's liturgy it is best to keep the entire liturgy as brief as possible, depending on the age of the children.

The choosing of the readings from scripture and possible readings other than scripture is very important. Much of the liturgy is verbal, and the verbal can pass completely above the heads of younger children if great care is not taken to present as much as possible of the verbal element in story form.

4) The next step is to discover with the community a way to respond to the scriptures in word and in deed. The active response should be symbolically expressed in the entrance, in the offering, in the symbols of the kiss of peace, etc. The response can take the form of gifts for the elderly, pictures of good deeds, tangible gifts for one another, e.g., rocks, papers, etc. The verbal responses during Mass should be sung, recited,

dramatized or danced. They can also be used as a "response" to the first reading.

5) The planner and the children could select a large variety of expressions or amplifications of the theme, e.g., scientific experiments, music, songs, rhythm bands, poems, stories, films, dramatizations, creative plays, puppets, dances, paintings, banners, posters, clay, papier-mache, arts and crafts involving cooking, hammering, sewing, etc. All these elements and many others have the possibility of a place in liturgy.

From this variety, one should *carefully* choose those especially prayerful and meaningful to the group. One should be extremely careful not to "clutter" a liturgy. *Simplicity is essential.*

6) The community should have one or more quiet and spontaneous prayer sessions related to the theme. These should be planned but not prestructured. Allow ample opportunity for the operation of the Holy Spirit. The group might sit in a circle for this prayer period, with hands joined and heads bowed in silent prayer. The leader may quietly and pensively contribute snatches of theme-related prayer phrases to direct the thinking of the group. After this the children should be *invited* to express their thoughts and prayers out loud. These thoughts should form the prayers used in the liturgy. As the children become more practiced, older children especially should compose all of their own prayers (with adult guidance as needed) e.g., penitential rite, opening prayers, prayers of the faithful, prayer over the gifts, closing prayer. These should be reviewed by the priest in accord with paragraph #51 of the *Directory.*

7) This step is one of the most important. The planner and children should prayerfully rethink the entire liturgy, eliminating all that is not pertinent; substituting, tying loose ends, etc., until there is a very consistent theme drawn throughout the liturgy with some concrete object to symbolize the main idea. The younger the children involved, the more concrete objects ought to be utilized. The one question that should be asked constantly is: Is this liturgy prayerful for these people?

8) Those parts of the liturgy in which the children are involved should be practiced to *relative* perfection. However, do not labor artful rendition to the point of turning children off, initiating exclusivity, or losing the spirit of prayer. Do not ask children to do things that are not natural to them, e.g., to read a lengthy or difficult selection out loud. Above all, children's liturgy must be an authentic act of worship for them. Children's liturgy belongs to children and God. Artful perfection is not to be expected, for the liturgy should be as smudgy and unpredictable as children are, but relative perfection is necessary for them to be able to truly celebrate even on their level.

9) Last of all, the liturgy outline should be written up and given to the

celebrant. The celebrant should have the liturgy form enough in advance so he can work on his homily and truly understand the liturgy. He also may have questions or suggestions which can be worked into the liturgy.

During this entire process, it is essential to remember that in the liturgy the children must touch God and be touched by God. At some point, at least, it must be possible to sense the presence of God and the union with one another in that presence. The liturgy, as a prayer form, must cause the children to become intensely serious about God, thus developing their relationship with God. The liturgy must cause each child to truly pray—to enter into union with God.

All the above steps may seem complicated and could leave some planners with a sense of defeat before they start. That is not at all necessary. A children's liturgy program begins slowly, and many of the steps outlined above will take a great deal of time to understand and put into practice. Eventually, the reluctant planners will find that it does not take as much time as they feared, once the children themselves are doing some of the work, and once they see the advantages of having the various sections besides religion class working on the same theme. In a school, the banners can be worked on during art classes, various nonscripture readings can be found during English class, and the plays can be part of drama class. One thing that is essential is that the children talk about *why* they are doing what they are doing, and come to an understanding of the liturgy and its various sections.

If and when a children's liturgy program becomes part of the real working of the parish and/or school, then the parents should be invited to attend Mass on the day that their children are doing the liturgy, and they will be pleasantly surprised. Eventually they can be brought into the workings of the liturgy itself. The younger the children, the more the parents can be asked to do things, but the parents of all ages are more willing than we often think they are to pray with their children.

After a few months of these liturgies, which will begin simply, the people involved should meet again and discuss how things are going. The creative teachers will have done much more than those whose talents lie in other directions, but if a spirit of exchange can be developed then good liturgies can be done by all the classes. The celebrant must be closely involved with all of this so that his own evaluation of what has been done can be given, and can be discussed. Special attention should be paid to the liturgies that have been very successful, and to those that have been especially bad, so that the lessons in each can be seen. In a period of about three or four months, a good solid program of children's liturgies can be well on the way to becoming an integral part of the spiritual program of the parish and/or school.

Chapter 3

ROLE OF THE PRIEST IN CHILDREN'S LITURGY

The role of the priest in liturgy has been and will continue to be the subject of countless books, talks, and articles. The theological and psychological aspects of "being celebrant" are so intimately tied to the essence of priesthood that many if not most priests are understandably nervous about even discussing the topic. Yet, it is a topic which must not only be discussed, it must be researched and debated, knowing full well that the role of the priest in the mystery of liturgy will never be fully understood.

In the interest of some brevity, this chapter will not deal with the role of the celebrant in general, nor with ministerial style—there are many available articles by more competent authors on those subjects. Rather, this chapter will try to zero in on the role of the priest in children's liturgy. Some background in liturgical style will be presumed.

I. The Role in Planning

The priest who intends to be involved with children's liturgy must know and understand modern liturgical principles and laws. Liturgy expresses the worship of the Church, not the tastes of the priest. Yet liturgy is not frozen; it must reflect the community as it is. The priest is the person who must deal with these two poles: universal Church and individual need. He must never become a slave to either one, or the liturgy will fail.

In order to do this, the priest must know well the principles of the universal liturgy and the laws of the Church; and also the specific nature and needs of the community, especially if those needs are different from his own needs (as is obviously the case in children's liturgy). In other words, being the priest in a children's liturgy requires much research and effort. If a priest is not willing or able to expend the effort, then he should not attempt children's liturgy. This is not one of those areas in life where poorly done is better than not done at all.

The research involved in understanding the needs of the community, especially children, includes so much it could never be listed. Besides the reading in psychology, sociology, etc., let us only make one strong recommendation for research—listening. A celebrant must have listened to his people and with his people before he has a right to speak.

Even before the actual preparation for liturgy, one critical role of the priest is catechesis. The *Directory for Masses with Children* stresses this in paragraph #12. This catechesis is for both children and parents, and its ultimate purpose is to create a climate with the community which allows good liturgy to happen. The priest is the teacher; he is to insure that the people are given the opportunity to learn not only what liturgy is, but also why. That is what liturgy is.

Once the priest is prepared with his research, and the parents and children are prepared by good catechesis, then the actual planning for liturgy can take place.

The role of the priest in planning liturgy changes constantly. Ultimately, he is a resource person and questioner. The children and adults should plan the Mass (see Chapter 2) and not necessarily the priest. But that does not mean the priest is left out. Others do the specific planning, while the priest is sort of on the sidelines, watching, coaching, helping—but not dominating. When a first or second draft of the liturgy is presented to him, he can question why things have been done a certain way, or explain why changes are needed. If there are unfinished parts of the liturgy which the planners wish the priest to finish, he can work on those areas. But it is not just his liturgy, or just someone else's liturgy—it is the liturgy of a community of which the priest is a vital part.

Two mistakes are often made. The first is when a priest works up a liturgy all by himself and brings it to a group and tells them to "do" it, as if it were a play. That is not liturgy, that almost is a play. The danger with any liturgy book which includes models, including this one, is that the models may be used for another celebration rather than as examples. Liturgy must be created by the group each time. The second mistake priests make is letting someone else plan the whole liturgy and then sitting in judgment on it according to his whims. No priest has the right to reject a liturgy presented to him without discussion and explanation. The explanation should contain elements of what the Church wants, not just what the priest likes or dislikes. Clerical liturgical tyranny, of either the left or the right, is outdated.

II. Role of the Priest in the Actual Celebration

"It is the responsibility of the priest who celebrates with children to make the celebration festive, fraternal, meditative. Even more than in Masses with adults, the priest should try to bring about this kind of spirit.

It will depend upon his personal preparation and his manner of acting and speaking with others" *(Directory for Masses with Children #23).*

The priest is in charge of the celebration, it is he who determines the mood, the spirit, the atmosphere. To say he is in charge does not mean he rules, rather, it means he serves. When a priest comes together with children to celebrate Jesus, to touch God, the priest determines what happens, that is part of what "priest" means liturgically. There are priests who understand this and make great and heroic effort to preside at the liturgy well, but others just "say Mass" practically unaware of their responsibility to those with whom they celebrate. Just exactly how the priest is in charge will become more clear as we examine how a priest presides at children's liturgy.

All of the preparation work has been done, and it is time to begin the celebration. At this point the priest must be comfortable with what will happen. If the entrance procession includes 30 children blowing soap bubbles, the priest should like soap bubbles; if 14 first-graders are linked together like a caterpillar, and the priest has agreed beforehand to be the 15th, this is no time to back out. The entrance rites set a tone, and atmosphere—the priest determines what this is. On the one hand, he must demand that the planners have planned an entrance, by gestures or song or something that conveys the mood, and, on the other hand, he must make sure he carries out that planning.

The same comments apply to the penitential rites, the prayers, the gospel, the offertory, etc.—the priest must exercise his role carefully and for a purpose. "Above all, the priest should be concerned about the dignity, clarity, and simplicity of his actions and gestures. In speaking to the children he should express himself so that he will be easily understood, while avoiding any childish style of speech" *(Directory for Masses with Children #23).*

There are a few other items which should be commented on:

1) *Liturgical law* — During the celebration, the prior research into law will have proved worthwhile. Almost all priests have been trained to believe that law, especially liturgical law, is important. But we need to truly know what the Church intends to teach us by her law, so that we can make sure it happens. That does not mean we are slaves to the law, but rather that we know how to adapt the law. A priest cannot "do his own thing" in either a liberal or conservative fashion at Mass, especially at children's liturgy. The children are going to attend many other Masses with many other priests, and no priest has a right to confuse their ability to celebrate in the future by being too intransigent or too slipshod now. In other words, when a priest makes the necessary adaptations, he should make the correct ones, to achieve the purpose of bringing Jesus and the children together.

2) *Reverence* — Reverence is an attitude of mind and body in which a person shows love and devotion. For a child that might mean moving around, singing, or even dancing. It probably is not being quiet or inactive. The average posture of a child is motion—therefore motion will play a part in his reverence. This may upset adults, it may take some getting used to by the priest, but it is essential.

On the other hand, there are still such things as noise (rather than good sound) and playing around. Children must learn that liturgy is not playtime, even though it is festive. When discipline is needed, those adults with the children, not the priest, should administer it.

3) *Furnitures and postures* — While most children's liturgies should be celebrated in church (if only to provide continuity between Sundays and weekdays), usually the church creates terrible problems. Flexibility is important, and churches have fixed altars, fixed pews, and many still have altar rails. These problems can be gotten around with some initiative, however. With grades one to three, the floor is the best place to be, for both children and priest. No matter what the priest's background, it is difficult for almost any priest to sit on the floor in full vestments for the first time, with 30 or more children sitting beside and on top of him. But once done, it will more easily be done again.

Other postures include: kneeling at various times, holding hands, especially during the Our Father (this is possible up to the sixth grade and again in the 11th or 12th, but not in between), having the whole congregation stand around the altar from the preface on, having children imitate the gestures of the priest, etc. All these postures are attempts to involve the children in what is happening and often they are in themselves sacramental. The specific purpose of the gesture, therefore, be it traditional or not, should be explained.

4) *The homily* — The homily is the specific moment of tying things together. The *Directory* does permit adults other than the priest to use this time (#24), but usually this is the special time of the celebrant.

The theme of the liturgy contained in the scriptures, prayers, songs, etc., should be drawn out and made real. It is difficult to do this, but especially difficult if the priest tries to preach at children. Even if they pay attention, they will rarely hear what is being told them. Real creativity is needed to accomplish a good homily with children.

If possible, talk with them. Ask questions, let them ask questions. Have the older students prepare statements about the scriptures. Use props, drawings, pictures, gestures, stories, plays, etc. Involve the children in a search for meaning in the scriptures. Let them preach to you. Walk around among them.

One technical detail: If a child gives an answer, the priest should

28

repeat it if necessary so all can hear it. Children talk softly, yet want to hear others. Also don't make the homily long; children's attention span is short. The priest should have a point to make, let it be made, then stop. The children should be able to tell anyone who asks later what the theme of the Mass was from the homily.

Conclusion

The role of the priest is difficult and critical. But most priests, with work, can learn to truly lead the children to touch God. The priest needs good planning, much personal preparation, prayer and good ministerial style.

Good ministerial style is more and more critically important as the inherent beauty and power of the revised rites come into view. The tone of voice, the use of gestures, eye contact, smiles, everything is part of creating the atmosphere. A priest can destroy the call, he can become a source of tension instead of a source of dynamic living with the God-man. A priest can rule liturgy instead of allowing liturgy to be celebrated.

The role of the celebrant is to lead, mediate, guide, call, inspire. All of these words mean that the priest indeed takes the place of Jesus Christ, and Jesus never imposed himself on others. He brought people out of themselves. By Baptism we have God within us, and the moment of liturgy is a moment of touching the God within us and within those around us, or receiving a Eucharist of word and sacrament which deepens what we already have. If the priest rules the liturgy, he does not admit our Baptism, our grace-filled personhood—he treats us as unbelievers, and he neither lets God come forth from us nor shares God with us. Communion then even becomes what the priest gives us, rather than a call to union with Jesus Christ to which we respond.

But it must be remembered that there is something more important than all these techniques, than all the style and actions and creative ideas put together—authenticity. Authenticity is another name for integrated sanctity. Children know truth and phoniness by instinct. The insincere priest who does everything right will fail to bring children to touch God; the authentic lover of children and God will bring children with him wherever he goes.

For any priest authenticity is a struggle which must always be waged. For those engaged in children's liturgy, the ability of children to be perceptive of sanctity is dangerous—it reminds one of the story of the Emperor's new clothes.

Chapter 4

FIVE MODEL LITURGIES FOR GRADES 1 AND 2

Introduction

In this chapter we present five model liturgies for grades one and two. They are independent of each other; each stands alone.

These five liturgies are fully developed prayer forms, the end result of dozens and dozens of other liturgies. They are not how a community begins, but rather what a community can do when it reaches some point along the way. They are not perfect by any means; there are mistakes in them, but they are an attempt.

They have been placed here in order that readers might see what is possible. They are not to be used as recipes. Even the children who created them and prayed them could not use them again; liturgy must be alive and freshly attuned to the community each time.

Some points will be noticed in these liturgies. First of all, they include more items than the liturgy outline form talked about in Chapter 2. During these liturgies the priest still has the outline form with him to tell him what to do, but the outline form is a skeleton. Liturgy goes beyond our ability to put it all down one way on paper.

Secondly, the "leader" who appears in many of the liturgies is the teacher or planner. The quasi-ministerial role taken by the leader (male or female) simplifies the role of the priest and is a great help to unite the preparation and the actual liturgy.

Thirdly, some of the liturgies look complicated and difficult to carry out. Starting from scratch they would be, but it must be remembered that a whole community of people has gotten to the point where doing these things comes naturally. Months of much simpler liturgies made these liturgies possible.

Fourthly, in some of these liturgies and in some in the other chapters, scripture paraphrases are given which could help the homilist understand how to present the actual scripture.

Fifthly, if Virginia Sloyan's criterion, quoted in Chapter 1 is correct, they worked. Children, to some extent, were more able to experience Jesus Christ. And so were the adults.

LITURGY I

Theme:

God is he in whom we live.

Symbol:

Water

Materials Needed:

One small Dixie cup for each child. (Each Dixie cup will contain a small amount of water. The water will be poured into the finger bowl at the Offering.)

One large container (preferably a transparent bowl) of water to be used in the center of the circle of children during the Thanksgiving.

A pitcher or large ladle to pour the water.

One small sponge for each child (about two inches square).

A towel to dry the children's hands after the Thanksgiving.

Sponge cake and juice for refreshments after the liturgy, if desired.

Preparation:

1) *Primary Preparation:*
   Give each child a tiny, colored, commercial sponge. Ask each child to make a face on his sponge and give it a name. Invite the children to play with their sponges in water, to make up stories about them, and to color pictures of them. Guide them to experience how the sponges feel and to express this feeling in dramatic play. Reflect with the children on how they live in God the way the sponges live in the ocean.

2) *Other Suggestions:*
   Provide as many experiences of water and water creatures as possible. Encourage the children to bring seashells, seaweeds, and water pets—goldfish, turtles, etc. Public libraries often have large colored pictures of water, water plants, and water animals, as well as many related scientific and fictional books, films, and filmstrips. *Fish Is Fish,*[1] an excellent book for children, illustrates well the necessity for fish to remain always in water. (Here is an opportunity to present the parallel need for us to remain always in God's love.) Related art and science projects done by the children, as well as real life, should decorate the celebration room. *The Sea*[2] is an excellent aid for helping adults and children learn how to share meditative prayer on this theme.

3) *Reflection:*
   (for planner and children)

   "There's a place for us. . ." sang Tony and Maria, in *West Side Story.*

   There's a place for each of us in God.

   In him we live and move and have our being.

   In him we are at home.

   In him our hearts find a place where they feel right.

   When we breathe, we breathe in his presence.

   When we smile, we smile in his face.

   When we open our eyes, we look into his eyes.

   And everywhere is beauty and love.

   And everywhere is God, close around us.

   "He is as close to us as the atmosphere we live in."

   Water is a natural, scriptural, and sacramental symbol. In the liturgy, water is used as a sign of preparing for the presence of Jesus. It reminds Christians of their Baptism and of how they are born into water and the Spirit and become open to God's grace.

THE LITURGY

Opening Song:

"*Come My Brothers*" to the tune of "*Michael Row the Boat Ashore*" (Use ballet-form hand and arm gestures.)[3]

In the opening song of this liturgy, we literally open our arms and invite all our brothers and sisters to come with us to worship the Lord in whose hands are the "oceans deep."

Greeting:

The celebrant opens his arms to welcome us. It reminds us of how God's arms are all around us just as the ocean is all around a sponge; and of how we should open our whole being to God.

Penitential Rite:

The children are seated comfortably and informally in a close group on the floor. The leader asks the children to close their eyes, bow their heads, and join hands with one another. The leader will read the Penitential Rite, asking the children to respond. Then the leader will invite the children to think of a time when they closed God out by hurting someone. If the children wish, they may express this out loud, with all the children responding.

For the times we have not been open to God. . .

For the times we have not been open to other people. . .

For the times we have not used water reverently and thankfully. . .

Response:

Jesus, we are sorry.

Prayer:

God, today you are teaching us that you are always all around us, just as the water is all around the sponge. Please help us always to be open to you. We ask this through Jesus Christ. . .

Scripture Reading:

Romans 8:9, 16, 35, 38, 39 (adapted)

The Spirit of God has made his home in you. If the Spirit of God has made his home in you, you are at home in the Spirit and you can call God: "Daddy." Nothing can shut us out from the love of Christ; even if we are troubled or worried, or being picked on, or don't have food or clothes, or are frightened or beat. I know for sure that neither death nor life, nothing in the whole world, nothing still to come, not any power, or force or anything can ever close us off from the love of God. We always are at home in God.

Additional Reading:

A Home in the Ocean[4]

The additional reading, *A Home in the Ocean,* shows how close water is to a sponge family. Yet, even though the water goes right into every pore of the sponges' bodies, the sponges did have an opportunity to choose to leave the ocean. God is always all around us, but we can choose to ignore his presence, or we can choose to be breathlessly present to his presence.

Gospel Acclamation:

"Allelu!"[5]

Gospel:

Matthew 14:22-23
See also: *The Little Boat That Almost Sank* (adaptation of Matthew 14:22-23 and Mark 6:45-51)[6]

In the gospel, Peter senses that Jesus can control the most powerful water. Because of this faith in Jesus, Peter steps out of the boat and

34

begins to walk to Jesus on the water. But then Peter chooses to take his eyes off Jesus and to look at the raging waters he is treading. Losing faith in Jesus, he begins to sink but Jesus draws him up and brings him to himself.

Homily—Suggestion:

We are at home in God as a sponge is at home in the ocean. When we are in difficult situations, like Peter in the storm, we should trust Jesus and ask him to help us. But all the time we must try to keep our eyes on Jesus and put our hands into his. How can we keep our eyes on Jesus and how can we put our hands into his? (Discuss.)

Prayer of the Faithful:

Suggestions:

For all the people who are suffering because they do not have enough water. . .

For all the people who have not found a place in God. . .

For all the people who have closed other people out of their lives. . .

Other needs. . .

Response:

Lord, hear our prayer.

(The children should be invited to add their own petitions.)

Offering:

Each child will bring a small container (Dixie cup, one-quarter full of water) and pour it into the finger bowl which the priest is holding for the priest to use in the liturgy to wash his hands.

Offertory Song:

"Put Your Hand in the Hand" (Use appropriate hand gestures.)[7]

Prayer Over the Gifts:

Lord, take our gifts of water, bread and wine. Help us always to use water, bread and wine as you want us to use them.

Holy, Holy, Holy:

(sung, if possible)

Eucharistic Prayer #2

Acclamation:

(Choose the one most familiar to the children.)

Amen:

(sung if possible, or applause)

Our Father:

(Join hands.)

Rite of Peace:

Each child will give his sponge to another child and say: "God be all around you."

Communion:

(Use both species where possible.)

Communion Song:

"The Children's Dance" from *Hansel and Gretel.*[8]

Thanksgiving:

(*This is especially important if the children did not receive Communion.*)

The children sit in a circle. The leader in a very soft, reverent, gentle, and intense voice sets an atmosphere of wonder and awe as he (or she) invites the children to be so quiet that they can hear God's word of joy in the water. The leader then pours water into a large container that has been placed in the center of the circle. The water is poured in such a way that the fall of the water is audible and the beauty of the flow can be observed. In complete silence the children allow their hands to play in the water, experiencing the soothing comfort of the Spirit present in his gifts of nature. This play is reverent, disciplined, truly contemplative, an act of worship.

Prayer:

God, you are always in us and around us just as the water is in and around the sponge. Help us to always surround other people with our care. Our care is your care. We are one.

Blessing:

Suggestion:

May God be all around you as the waters of the ocean are all around the sponge;

And may you always be open to God as the sponge is open to the waters of the ocean.

May your eyes be always on the Lord;

And may God bless you and hold your hand always in his hand.

In the name of the Father and of the Son, and of the Holy Spirit.

Closing Song:

(to the tune of *"He's Got the Whole World in His Hands"*)

He's got the slooshy, slurpy sponges in his hands. . .

He's got the great big ocean in his hands. . .

He's got you and me in his hands. . .

He's got the whole world in his hands. . .

Refreshments:

Sponge cake, juice; coffee for adults.

References:

1. *Fish Is Fish,* Leo Lionni, Pantheon, 201 E. 50th, New York, N.Y., 10022.

2. *The Sea,* Rod McKuen, San Sebastian Strings, Warner Bros., Inc., 4000 Warner Boulevard, Burbank, California 91505.

3. *"Come My Brothers"* (tune - *"Michael Row the Boat Ashore").*

4. *A Home in the Ocean,* part of the *Religious Awareness Reading Program.* Max Odorff, Crocus Books, Terrace Heights, Winona, Minnesota 55987.

5. "Allelu!" Ray Repp, F.E.L. Publications, Ltd., 1925 Pontius Avenue, Los Angeles, California 90025.

6. *The Little Boat That Almost Sank,* Arch Books, Concordia Publishing House, 3558 Jefferson Avenue, St. Louis, Missouri 63118.

7. "Put Your Hand in the Hand," Gene MacLellan. Copyright 1970, Beechwood Music Corp., Hollywood, California, currently found on various albums.

8. *Hansel and Gretel,* Disneyland Records, 477 Madison Avenue, New York, N.Y. 10022.

LITURGY II

Theme:

God is with us.

Symbol:

Fire

Materials Needed:

One waxed Dixie cup or milk carton as candle mold for each child.

One wick or candle remnant with wick for each child; wax for candles.

Colored crayon to melt in wax for colored candles; large container for a fire. The container for the fire should be of heavy metal, lined with aluminum foil. Grains of incense might be added for the symbolic fragrance and smoke.

Cupcakes decorated with lighted candles and juice for refreshments, if desired.

Each child has a prayer written on paper to be burned at the Thanksgiving.

Preparation:

1) *Primary Preparation:*
   By having the children make the candles themselves, each child experiences a share in the power to melt hard, cold wax. Later they observe that they really can literally make light in the world through their own work and the gifts of nature "which earth has given and human hands have made," as they see their candles lighting the altar.

   Each child can bring this sign to spiritual reality when he gives his candle with a good tiding to some old, perhaps "sad, lonely and cold" person. Wax for making the candles can be purchased from a craft shop. Children enjoy watching the wax melt in a heavy saucepan. The children need to be instructed to be very careful and to keep a safe distance from the hot wax. Lots of newspaper should be used to cover work areas. Each child can carefully hold his candle remnant or wick in the waxed container as the melted wax is being poured. Candle remnants are much easier than wicks for the children to manage. The candle remnants or wicks must be held straight and steady until the wax is at least partially hardened. After the candles are cool and hard the waxed container can be removed.

2) *Other Suggestions:*
   Provide the children with as many experiences of light and fire as possible. A bonfire with hot dogs or marshmallows followed by a songfest

around the fire would help the children experience the physical properties as well as the social potential of fire in building friendship, sharing, and unity. You might want to have the children play a game with a blindfold to help them experience how helpless they are without light. Procure films, filmstrips, or large colored pictures of the sun, stars, light, or fire. If you are in a safe place, you may wish to try a variation of the Thanksgiving suggested in this liturgy. Give each child a sparkler. Light one of the sparklers and have each child pass his light to the next child.

3) *Reflection:*
(for planner and children)

Fire is bright, vibrant, creative, energizing, dynamic and powerful; lighting the world, warming the world, and giving the world energy and life.

God is with us, and in us—bright, vibrant, creative, energizing, dynamic, and powerful; lighting our minds, warming our hearts, giving us life and love.

Fire has been a worship symbol from the earliest times. This symbolism is well developed in the Old Testament as well as in the New Testament and is part of every liturgy today. This liturgy focuses on fire as a symbol of energy, presence, love and inspiration to others.

You may wish to have the church darkened for the first part of the liturgy, or you may wish to have it darkened as the children bring their candles at the Offering.

THE LITURGY

Opening Song:

"Here We Are"[1]

In the opening song we bask in the warmth of one another's presence and express a desire to keep this fire of love kindled with care.

Greeting:

The celebrant in some way wishes the children a day filled with light, warmth, and love and the children warmly return the greeting.

Penitential Rite:

The children are seated comfortably and informally in a close group on the floor. The leader asks the children to close their eyes, bow their heads, and join hands with one another. The leader will read the Penitential Rite, asking the children to respond. Then the leader will invite the children to think of a time when they made the world less light and less warm by hurting someone. If the children wish, they may express this aloud, with all the children responding.

For the times we have not been a light of love and goodness to other people. . .

For the times we have not seen the light of love and goodness in other people. . .

For the times we have shut out God's light. . .

Response:

Jesus, we are sorry.

Prayer:

Dear God, you give us light and warmth and energy so that we can see the good world and be happy. Help us always to see your love in everything. This we ask through Jesus Christ. . .

Scripture Reading:

Ephesians 5:9-11, 14, 15, 20 (adapted)

You were darkness once, but now you are light in the Lord; be like children of light—always good, living right, and being truthful. Try to discover what the Lord wants of you, and have nothing to do with the works of darkness and Christ will shine on you. So be very careful about how you live; like intelligent and not like senseless people. Be filled with the Spirit and go on singing to the Lord in your hearts, so that always and everywhere you are giving thanks to God who is our Father in the name of our Lord Jesus Christ.

Optional Reading:

The Boy Who Listened to Fire[2]

God is with us all the time. We can say to God what Michael in the additional reading says to the fire, "You're here all around us by day and by night . . . the fire that warms us and gives us our light." Michael sat very quietly and listened to the fire. The fire told Michael about itself. If we are quiet and listen very carefully for God, we can hear God in the warmth of our hearts. God will tell us much about himself.

Response:

(to the tune of "God Is Love," by Father Clarence Rivers)[3]

God is fire;
And he is all full of light;
And full of warmth and energy.

Gospel Acclamation:

"Allelu!"[4]

40

Gospel:

Matthew 5:14-16

Homily:

Suggestion:

We can hear the presence of God in the quiet warmth of our hearts. We can hear God in the warm words of people. We can hear God in the warmth and light of his word in the liturgy. How? (Discuss.) When we receive Communion, we will hear Jesus in our hearts in a very special way. This presence of God has to shine in us like a light so that everyone can see that God is with us. How can we help others to see and hear the presence of God? (Discuss.)

Prayer of the Faithful:

Suggestions:

For all the people who are suffering because they do not have warm homes and warm clothes. . .

For the people who are sad and lonely and cold in their hearts. . .

For the people who do not know and love the light of God. . .

Other needs. . .

Response:

Lord, hear our prayer.

(The children should be invited to add their own petitions.)

Offering:

Each child will bring to the altar table a lighted candle that he himself made as a sign of his commitment to be a light to the world. Leave candles on altar. You may wish to have the church darkened for the Offering procession.

Offertory Song:

"We Are the Light of the World"[5]

Prayer Over the Gifts:

Lord, take our fire of love with the bread and wine, and keep our hearts and minds and bodies burning with love for you and for others.

Preface:

(Use simplest preface possible.)

Holy, Holy, Holy:

(sung, if possible)

Eucharistic Prayer:

#2

Acclamation:

(Use one most familiar to the children and sing, if possible.)

Amen:

(sung, or applause)

Our Father:

(Join hands and feel in one another's hands a sign of the warmth of God's love.)

Rite of Peace:

Handshake and greeting: "Peace be with you. Be a light!"

Communion:

(Use both species where possible.)

Communion Song:

"Those Who See Light"[6]

Thanksgiving:

The children will sit in a circle with hands joined. In the center of the circle will be a large container. The leader, in a very soft, reverent, gentle and intense voice sets an atmosphere of wonder and awe as he (or she) invites the children to be so quiet that they can hear God's word of warmth and care in the fire. Each child will give the celebrant a message of love he has written to God. The celebrant will place the message in the container. A fire will be started in the container by one of the children's candles. The children will listen to the fire in silent prayer. If the children so desire, they may pray their acts of love aloud. It may be good to have the children pass a flame to one another around the circle. Each child may say a prayer silently or aloud as he is holding the flame.

Prayer:

God, thank you for the fire of your love. Help us to be always warmly near other people, listening carefully to them and being very kind to them.

The celebrant, assuring us that the Lord is with us, opens his arms to show us how much Jesus wants us to come to him and be warmed in his love.

Blessing:

Suggestion:

May God shine in your mind with the light of his love;
And may he burn in your heart with the warmth of his life.
May you always hear God in the warmth of your heart;
And in the warm words of other people.
In the name of the Father, and of the Son, and of the Holy Spirit.

Closing Song:

"This Little Light of Mine"[7]

Refreshments:

Cupcakes decorated with lighted candles, juice; coffee for adults.

References

1. "Here We Are," Ray Repp, F.E.L. Publications, Ltd., 1925 Pontius Avenue, Los Angeles, California 90025.

2. "The Boy Who Listened to Fire," part of the *Religious Awareness Reading Program,* Max Odorff, Crocus Books, Terrace Heights, Winona, Minnesota 55987.

3. "God Is Love," Father Clarence Rivers.

4. "Allelu!" Ray Repp, F.E.L. Publications, Ltd., 1925 Pontius Avenue, Los Angeles, California 90025.

5. "We Are the Light of the World," Jean Anthony Greif, Vernacular Hymns, Publ.

6. "Those Who See Light," unknown.

7. "This Little Light of Mine," lyrics and melody traditional; World Library Publications, Inc., 2145 Central Parkway, Cincinnati, Ohio 45214.

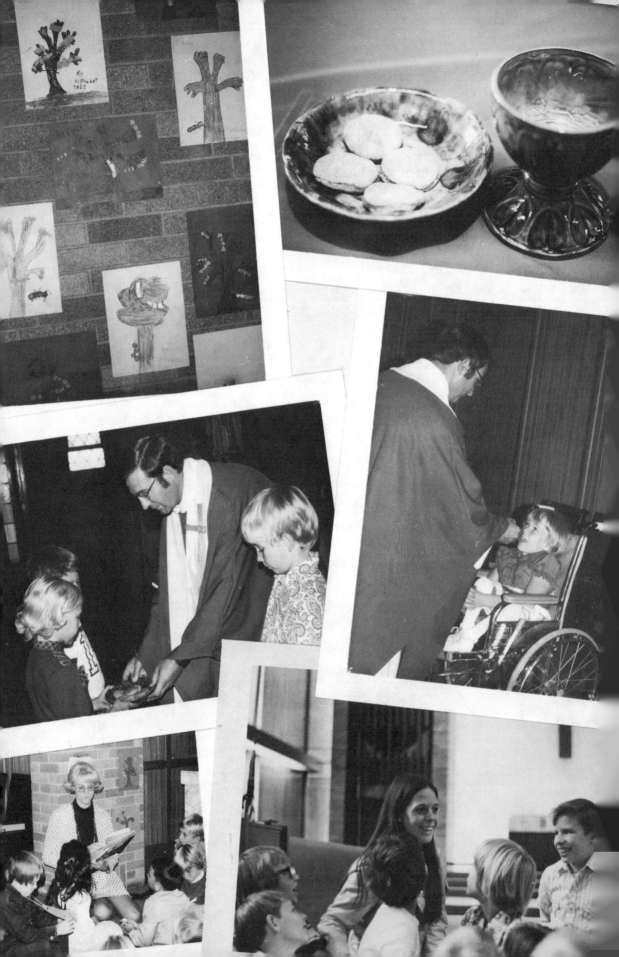

LITURGY III

Theme:

God is constantly renewing all things.

Symbol:

Wind

Materials Needed:

One balloon for each child to be filled with his own life breath before the liturgy. One bottle of commercial soap bubbles complete with some type of wand for making the bubbles.

Preparation:

1) *Primary Preparations:*

The dramatic recitation of James Weldon Johnson's "Creation," using ballet-form hand and arm movements, would be a good beginning. This poem is available in a beautifully illustrated book from Hallmark. Ask the children to join in on the words, "And God said, 'That's good.'" Then ask the children if they would like to form something with their very own life breath. Give each child an opportunity to blow a soap bubble, carefully pointing out to the children that none of these bubbles would ever come to be without their choosing to make them. Give a balloon to each child. Invite him to print his name or draw his face on the balloon if he would like. These balloons will be presented in the offering at the liturgy. The children's gift in the liturgy will be completed later when they bring these same balloons to lonely people, sharing with others their very own life breath.

2) *Other Suggestions:*

Each child might make a pinwheel. These should be artistically placed in the celebration room with a fan placed to activate them. The children might also like to make balloon animals, mobiles, etc. Provide as many wind experiences as possible. It would be interesting for the children to keep a weather chart for a week, observing the variation in wind. Try science experiments with air and wind, and view science filmstrips on the wind. Wind is also a good topic for dramatic play and art. There is a large selection of poems about the wind. Robert Louis Stevenson's poem, "The Wind," is also in song form.[1] A filmstrip, *Gilberto and the Wind,*[2] describes a little boy's experience with the wind.

3) *Reflection:*
(for planner and children)

Today God is creating the world.

Today God is calling all people and all things into being.
Today God expects each of us to help create new life in people.
We cannot force new life in people;
    we can only gently breathe into people the breath of love.
God looks at all that he makes and says: "That's good."
When we look at people with love and think: "You're good,"
we cause the other person to feel good about himself—
to want to be good—
    then we are breathing new life into that person.
But causing another person to come to new life in God demands steady,
    gentle, patient giving of life breath.
We can see an analogy of this in blowing a soap bubble.
If we control our breath,
    and blow in a steady, gentle, long stream,
    the bubble will become huge;
    but it's hard to use so much breath
    in a long, steady, gentle stream.
Creating new life in others requires gentleness,
    patience, endurance, and much self-control.
Today we celebrate God creating the world.
Today we celebrate God calling all people and things into being.
Today we celebrate our participation in helping to create new life in
    people.
Today we celebrate being fully alive.

THE LITURGY

Opening Song:

"Alive, Alive"[3]
In the opening song we join hands and form a large circle, asking one another to help us "learn a lot together; and it might be fun, seeing what the world's about and what the Lord has done." Perhaps the celebrant and children will want to blow soap bubbles as they enter.

Greeting:

The celebrant welcomes the children with some gesture and the children reciprocate. The celebrant and children may wish to clap their hands to express their joy in being together to celebrate the liturgy.

Penitential Rite:

The children are seated comfortably and informally in a close group on the floor. The leader asks the children to close their eyes, bow their heads, and join hands with one another. The leader will read the Penitential Rite, asking the children to respond. Then the leader will invite the children to think of a time when they were closed to the Spirit of God. If they wish, they may express this out loud with all the children responding.

> For the times we have not played with God . . .
> For the times we have hurt other people in our play . . .
> For the times we have left other people out of our play . . .

Response:

Jesus, we are sorry.

Prayer:

God, today you are showing us that you are like a playful wind—hard to see and yet always with us. Please help us always to play with you. We ask this . . .

Scripture Reading:

Genesis 2:5-7

The first scripture reading tells us that God breathes into us his very own life breath and we come to be. At the time when God made earth and heaven there was as yet no wild bush on the earth, nor was there any man to work the soil. However, a flood was rising from the earth and watering all the surface of the soil. God fashioned man of dust from the soil. Then he breathed into him the breath of life, and man became a living being.

Optional Reading:

The Wind and the Dwarfs[4]
In the additional reading, the dwarfs reject many childhood pleasures in order to choose, instead, the wind, a constant friend who would be always with them, helping them to play.

Response:

(to the tune of "Blowin' in the Wind," by Bob Dylan)[5]

Leader—How many times must I call to you, Before you know that I'm near?

All sing—The answer, my friend, is blowin' in the wind; the answer is blowin' in the wind.

Leader—How many times must I call to you, Before you come out to play?

All sing—as above.

Leader—How many times must I call to you, Before you know that I'm here?

All sing—as above.

Gospel Acclamation:

Sing "Allelu!"[6]

Gospel:

Matthew 19:13-15.
The Gospel tells us that Jesus was with the children; that he touched them; and that he blessed them.

Homily:

Suggestion:

God brings each of us into being every second with his own life breath. He is constantly breathing in us. Jesus brought the little children close around him. He touched them and played with them. He shared himself with them. He *chose* to do this even when others tried to tell him not to do it. Jesus, God, is always with us to give us new life, to play with us, and to share himself with us. But like the dwarfs, we always have to keep choosing him. We can't get so taken up with candy and raisins, and silver and gold, and milk and honey that we forget to love Jesus and to play with the Spirit of God.

Prayer of the Faithful:

Suggestions:

For all the people who do not find joy in their lives . . .
For all the people who do not play their lives honestly . . .
So that we will always serve you with joy and be moved by your
    pleasure . . .

Response:

Lord, hear our prayer.
(The children should be invited to add their own petitions.)

Offering:

Each child will give the celebrant a balloon filled with his own life breath. Later the children will bring these gifts of life and Spirit to poor children, shut-ins, or old people. Basket or box should be provided to hold balloons.

Offertory Song:

"Spirit of God."[7]

Prayer Over the Gifts:

Take our balloons, Lord, with our bread and wine, as a sign of our joy to be with you and help us always to be filled with the breath of your love.

Preface:

(Pick one that expresses God's power and love.)

Holy, Holy, Holy:

(sung, if possible)

Eucharistic Prayer:

#2

Acclamation:

(Choose the one most familiar to the children, singing if possible.)

Amen:

(Sung)

Our Father:

(Join hands.)

Rite of Peace:

Each child blows lightly on the forehead of another child and says: "The life of the Spirit be with you."

Communion:

(Use both species where possible.)

Communion Song:

"Run and Catch the Wind"[8]

Thanksgiving:

The children will sit in a circle with hands joined and heads bowed in silent prayer. The leader in a very soft, reverent, gentle and intense voice sets an atmosphere of wonder and awe as he (or she) invites the children to be so quiet that they can hear God's word of love and joy in their own breathing. Each child, in turn, will come to the center of the circle and devoutly blow a bubble (using a commercial bubble solution) to show that just as a beautiful bubble is formed by his breath from a shapeless glob, so we are made beautiful by the shaping breath (will) of God.

Prayer:

God, thank you for giving us life and making us happy and glad to be alive. Help all of us to run with you and "catch the wind." We ask this . . .

Blessing:

Suggestions:

When you breathe, may you breathe in God's breath;
And when you smile, may you smile in his face;
When you open your eyes, may you look into his eyes;
And may you see everywhere the goodness of creation.
In the name of the Father, and of the Son, and of the Holy Spirit.

Closing Song:

As an appropriate expression of the presence of the Spirit with us, the children will join hands and form a circle. The leader will be in the center. All will sing, "The Spirit Plays With Us" to the tune of "The Farmer in the Dell." Each child, in turn, will come to the center while the group sings, "The Spirit plays with (e.g.,) John . . ." After each child has had a turn, the group sings, "The Spirit plays with us . . ." while clapping.

Refreshments:

Sugar-blowin'-in-the-wind (commonly called cotton candy), a bubbly drink, bubble gum.

References

1. *A Child's Garden of Verses,* Disneyland Records, 477 Madison Avenue, New York 10022.

2. *Gilberto and the Wind,* Etc., Weston Woods Studios, Weston, Connecticut 06880.

3. "Alive, Alive," Album #2 of the *Life, Love, Joy* series, Silver Burdett, General Learning Corporation, Morristown, New Jersey 07960.

4. *The Wind and the Dwarfs,* part of the *Religious Awareness Reading Program,* Max Odorff, Crocus Books, Terrace Heights, Winona, Minnesota 55987.

5. A takeoff on "Blowin' in the Wind," Bob Dylan.

6. "Allelu!" Ray Repp, F.E.L. Publications, Ltd., 1925 Pontius Avenue, Los Angeles, California 90025.

7. "Spirit of God," Sister Miriam Therese Winter, Vanguard Music Corp., 250 West 57th Street, New York, New York 10019.

8. *Up With People,* Moral Re-Armament, Inc., 833 S. Flower Street, Los Angeles, California 90017.

LITURGY IV

Theme:

God is the beauty we discover in others.

Symbol:

Hidden treasure

Materials Needed:

One treasure box for each child, no bigger than a cigar box. Each child should get his own.

Preparation:

1) Primary Preparation:

Give each child a paper towel. With a black magic marker, make a mark on each child's paper towel. Have each child dampen his paper towel and watch all the beautiful colors that were hidden in the black spread out across his paper towel. Talk with the children about the secret beauties they have discovered in others. Ask them to think of ways that they could give some of their hidden beauty—love and thoughtfulness—to others. Invite the children to decorate a hidden treasure box in which they can keep their hidden treasures, e.g., a smile, a kind word, picking things up from the floor, etc. In the Offering of the Mass, the children will bring their secret treasure boxes. Only God will be able to see what is in the box; only people who see with their hearts will be able to see the gems of beauty that the children brought forth in others by their little acts of thoughtfulness.

2) Reflection:

(for planner)

No one is a one-level house; no one is even a split-level; each one is a labyrinth. Each person who comes into another's life comes in by a different way and finds inside a different treasure. How many treasures are waiting to be found in the secret places of every person's heart! There is within the human heart a treasure-in-process for everyone, but the treasure is not fully in existence until the other looks on it with love, fulfilling God's creative act. The number of treasures to be found in a person is limited only by the number of persons who come to look with love at the treasures. God is the secret beauty, the treasure hidden in the house of another person, waiting to be discovered. If we do not discover the beauty in others, it may never be discovered, for each facet of a person requires a special other to unlock the closed doors and the fastened windows.

THE LITURGY

Opening Song:

"Come Out!"[1] (with appropriate actions)
In the opening song we sing about how we see God "in the morning light . . . in my brother's eyes . . . in the whole wide world . . . if only I try . . ."

Greeting:

At the beginning of the liturgy the priest opens his arms to show us that Jesus and all the Christian community wants us to come in, to open our hearts, and to feel safe and free with the community of Jesus.

Penitential Rite:

The children are seated comfortably and informally in a close group on the floor. The leader asks the children to close their eyes, bow their heads, and join hands with one another. The leader will read the Penitential Rite, which the children, as a group, composed. Then the leader will invite the children to think of a time when they closed their eyes to the beauty of someone because they were angry or upset with that person. If the children wish, they may express this aloud, with all the children responding.

For the times we have not treated other persons as God's living place . . .
For the times we have been closed to other people . . .
For the times we have not seen beauty in other people . . .

Response:

Jesus, we are sorry.

Prayer:

Dear God, you made each person very special. You hid a secret treasure of yourself in each person. Please help us to take care of your treasure and to share it with other people. We ask this . . .

Scripture Reading:

Sirach 6:14-17 (adapted)
In the first scripture reading we are told that a friend who always sees the beauty in us no matter what happens is a rare treasure.
A faithful friend is a sure shelter,
    whoever finds one has found a rare treasure.
A faithful friend is something beyond price,
    there is no measuring his worth.
A faithful friend is the comfort of life, and
    those who serve the Lord will find one.

Whoever serves the Lord makes true friends,
for if you are a good person, you will have a good friend.

Additional Reading:

The Secret House[2]
The additional reading, *The Secret House,* shows the endless pleasant surprises waiting in a house that, at first appearance, seemed frightening and unfriendly.

Response:

(to the tune of "Blowin' in the Wind")

Sing—A secret, my friend, is hidden in all men;
A secret is hidden in all men.

Leader—Spontaneous recitation, e.g.,
God has a special love for each of us that is all our own and nobody else's. We each want to use our special gift of love in a special way for other people.

Sing—For Jesus, my friend, is hidden in all men, for Jesus is hidden in all men.

Gospel Acclamation:

"Allelu!"[3]

Gospel:

Luke 19:2-10
See also: *The Great Surprise* Luke 19:2-10 (adapted)[4]
In the gospel Jesus recognizes the good in a man the other people do not like.

Homily:

Suggestion:

The kingdom of God is the treasure hidden in each person. That treasure is worth more than all the riches of the world. That treasure contains the whole mystery of Jesus. We have to make other people feel so safe and so accepted and so "housed" in our love that they can show us all the cobwebs and dust and coverings they have used to hide their treasures. For small children it will be necessary to use specific examples of people who seem ugly and frightening but who are really beautiful.

Prayer of the Faithful:

So that we may find, bring out, and share the hidden beauty of God that is in our own selves . . .

So that we may help other people to discover the hidden beauty in themselves . . .

For those who do not know the beauty of God's secrets . . .

(The children should be invited to add their own petitions.)

Response:

Lord, hear our prayer.

Offering:

Each child will bring a treasure box symbolic of a secret gift he will give to someone, e.g., a smile, setting the table, picking up papers, a kind word, etc.

Offertory Song:

"Zacchaeus"[5]

Prayer Over the Gifts:

Bless our gifts of bread and wine and our hidden treasures of love, Lord. May we always share your love with others, through Christ our Lord.

Preface:

(Use simplest one possible.)

Holy, Holy, Holy:

(sung, if possible)

Eucharistic Prayer:

#2

Acclamation:

(Choose the one most familiar to the children and sing, if possible.)

Amen:

(Sung, or applause.)

Our Father:

(Join hands.)

Rite of Peace:

Each child will whisper to another child Jesus' beautiful treasure of peace.

Communion:

(under both species, if possible)

Communion Song:

"God Made Us All"[6]

Thanksgiving:

The children sit in a circle. The leader in a very soft, reverent, gentle, and intense voice sets an atmosphere of wonder and awe as he (or she) invites the children to be so quiet that they can hear God speak to them in the silence of their minds, in the hidden places of their hearts. (A few moments are allowed for silent prayer.)

Closing Prayer:

God, you keep the secret of your tremendous love hidden from proud people and show it to us, your little ones. Help us always to look for your love in everything in the whole world, especially in the people you make. We ask . . .

Blessing:

Suggestions:

May you open your hearts to the treasures of God's love;
And may you treasure the beauty of his love within your heart.
May you show forth the treasures of love hidden deep within others;
And may others bring to light the beauty of you.
And may God bless you in the name of the Father, and of the Son, and
    of the Holy Spirit.

Closing Song:

"Everything Is Beautiful"[7]

Refreshments:

Cookies with a secret message from scripture hidden inside, juice; coffee for the adults.

References

1. *Come Out!* Jack Miffleton, World Library Publications, Inc., 2145 Central Parkway, Cincinnati, Ohio 45214.

2. *The Secret House,* part of the *Religious Awareness Reading Program,* Max Odorff, Crocus Books, Terrace Heights, Winona, Minnesota 55987.

3. "Allelu!" Ray Repp, F.E.L. Publications, Ltd., 1925 Pontius Avenue, Los Angeles, California 90025.

4. *The Great Surprise,* Mary Warren, Arch Books, Concordia Publishing House, 3558 Jefferson Avenue, St. Louis, Missouri 63118.

5. *Joy Is Like the Rain,* Sister Miriam Therese Winter, Medical Mission Sisters, Vanguard Music Corporation, 250 West 47th Street, New York, New York 10019.

6. *Come Out!* Jack Miffleton, World Library Publ., Inc., 2145 Central Parkway, Cincinnati, Ohio 45214.

7. *Everything Is Beautiful,* Ray Stevens, Barnaby Records, 816 North Lacienda Boulevard, Los Angeles, California 90069.

LITURGY V

Theme:

God is the extravagant giver.

Symbol:

Surprises

Materials Needed:

Each child should bring one gift that is special to him to give at the Offering and to give away later in the day; and a small gift that he made to give to another child at the sign of peace. One small religious gift for the celebrant to give to the children at the Thanksgiving.

Preparation:

1) *Primary Preparation:*
In having the children make small gifts to give to one another, stress the importance of their putting their whole selves into the gift and of filling the making of their gifts with feelings of peace. Talk with the children about the extravagance of love.

2) *Reflection:*
(for planner)

St. Francis of Assisi gives us a beautiful example of the extravagance of love. He gave all and suffered rejection and humiliation with an exuberant and laughing heart. The song of the men in the fiery furnace is an example of the extravagance of love. The cross of Jesus Christ is the ultimate example of the extravagance of love. Over and over again in our lives we are surprised by the extravagance of God's personal love for none other than ourselves. But repeatedly the love of God surprises us, confuses us, challenges us, humbles us, and purifies us. The extravagance of God's love can only be accepted as a surprise in faith, for it is a shock and a stumbling block to human rationale and human bargaining.

The place of celebration should look like a hall of surprises, well decorated with mobiles, streamers, ribbons, pinatas, hats for the children, etc. The Hill of Surprise (the table of the Eucharist) should appropriately be the center of attention.

THE LITURGY

Opening Song:

"Do, Re, Mi"[1]

Greeting:

Spontaneous by celebrant, who should set a tone of wonder and surprise.

Penitential Rite:

The children should be seated comfortably in an informal group. After reading the Penitential Rite and allowing time for the children to respond, the leader should invite the children to think of a time when they were selfish and would not share with others. If they wish, the children may express this out loud.

For the times we did not give ourselves to others. . .

For the times we did not give ourselves to you. . .

For the times we have been jealous of other people's gifts. . .

Response:

Jesus, we are sorry.

Prayer:

Dear God, every day is a new day. Every moment is a surprise from you. Help us always to be glad for everything that happens to us. We ask. . .

Scripture Reading:

1 Corinthians 2:7, 9, 16; Jeremiah 3:19, 22 (adapted)

From the beginning God has been preparing for us a tremendous surprise. In the first scripture reading, we hear that the surprise has been promised us, if we will but run the race with all our strength and all our hearts. The greatest surprise of all—God wants us to call him Father. "The secret of God is that, before the world began, he chose to make us share in his glory—the things that no eye has seen and no ear has heard, things beyond the mind of man, all that God has prepared for those who love him.

And I was thinking:

How I wanted to place you with my sons, and give you a country of delights, the best home in all the world. I had thought you would call me: My father, and would never stop following me.

Who can know the mind of the Lord? But we are those who have the mind of Christ.

We are here, we are coming to you, for you are our God."

Optional Reading:

The Hall of Surprises[2]
In the optional reading, we see the world as a place of never-ending change. Throughout our lives, if we are open, we constantly are making new discoveries; we have new insights; even our very value system is gradually but amazingly transformed. In the end, we are surprised to find that the slowest as well as the fastest win the race.

Response:

"The Sound of Music"[3]
(Sing as many verses as you wish, or play the record and sing with it.)

Gospel Acclamation:

Recorded yodel refrain from *The Lonely Goatherd*[4]
(In this liturgy use either response or Gospel acclamation, not both.)

Gospel:

Matthew 20:1-16
See also: *Sir Abner and His Grape Pickers* (Matthew 30:1-16)[5]
In the gospel we see the surprising generosity of God to those who did not hear the call of God until late.

Homily:

Suggestion:

All the scripture readings say that our values, the world's values, are not God's values. They point up the folly of looking for the kingdom on a safe and sure road. Rather, true values are to be discovered in risk, surprise, and change. Our love cannot be calculating and half-hearted, but bold and generous. A second-grader writes: "We are one in God's way. We are very, very special in God's way. Do you know why we are one in God's way? Because he loves the whole world and we all love God. I know that some people do not know about God. And they have a lot of money. And yet they are still poor because they do not know about God." This is a time to explore with children true values.

Prayer of the Faithful:

Suggestions:

So that we will always use all of our gifts in the service of God. . .

So that we will always be thankful for whatever God gives us. . .

For those who do not have as many gifts as we have. . .

Response:

Lord, hear our prayer.
(The children should be invited to share their petitions.)

Offering:

Each child will bring a favorite something, e.g., a toy, and offer to God gladness and joy for this "surprise" from him. These surprises will be given to poor children later.

Offertory Song:

"My Favorite Things"[6]

Prayer Over the Gifts:

Bless the gifts we give to you, Lord, for you first have given all good gifts to us. May we always share your gifts with others.

Preface:

(Use one that stresses God's wonder and goodness.)

Holy, Holy, Holy:

(sung, if possible)

Eucharistic Prayer:

#2

Acclamation:

(Choose one that is most familiar to the children; sung, if possible.)

Amen:

(sung)

Our Father:

(Join hands.)

Rite of Peace:

Each child will give a surprise peace offering that he made to another child.

Communion:

(Use both species where possible.)

Communion Song:

"A Bell Is Just a Bell"[7]

Thanksgiving:

The children sit in a circle. The leader, in a very soft, reverent, gentle, and intense voice sets an atmosphere of wonder and awe as he (or she) invites the children to be very quiet so that they can hear the love of God all around them. The celebrant gives each child a small religious gift, e.g., a cross pin, as a sign of God's gifts to us.

Prayer:

God, you give us so many surprises of your love.

Please help us to surprise other people and to make them happy. We ask. . .

Blessing:

Suggestion:

May you always be filled with wonder and surprise at the goodness of God to you;

May you fill others with wonder and surprise at your goodness to them;

May the whole world be a constant surprise to you and may you see the mystery of God everywhere.

And may you finally see the face of God himself.

In the name of the Father, and of the Son, and of the Holy Spirit.

Closing Song:

"Edelweiss"[8]

Refreshments:

Orange soda and cherry popsicles; coffee for adults.

References

1. *The Sound of Music,* Rodgers and Hammerstein, Disneyland Records, 477 Madison Avenue, New York, New York 10022.

2. *The Hall of Surprises,* part of the *Religious Awareness Reading Program,* Max Odorff, Crocus Books, Terrace Heights, Winona, Minnesota 55987.

3. *The Sound of Music,* Rodgers and Hammerstein, Disneyland Records, 477 Madison Avenue, New York, New York 10022.

4. *The Sound of Music,* Rodgers and Hammerstein, Disneyland Records, 477 Madison Avenue, New York, New York 10022.

5. *Sir Abner and His Grape Pickers,* Janice Kramer, Arch Books, Concordia Publishing House, 3558 Jefferson Avenue, St. Louis, Missouri 63118.

6. *The Sound of Music,* Rodgers and Hammerstein, Disneyland Records, 477 Madison Avenue, New York, New York 10022.

7. "A Bell Is Just a Bell," Kevin Boos, St. Anthony's Parish Hymnal, Pocatello, Idaho 83201.

8. *The Sound of Music,* Rodgers and Hammerstein, Disneyland Records, 477 Madison Avenue, New York, New York 10022.

Chapter 5

EIGHT COMMUNITY LITURGIES — A COORDINATED SET FOR GRADES 2, 3 and 4

Introduction:

These eight liturgies represent the result of an attempt to plan an entire series to develop one set of concepts over a long period of time.

This is definitely an advanced form of liturgical development, but a valid goal. Any one of the liturgies could stand alone, but taken together they are very similar to what the adult Church has always done with the Church year, the development of Holy Week, and the Christmas and Easter cycles. Children who experienced this coordinated set of liturgies waited eagerly for the next step in the progression to Christmas, and then the reminder of it all at Easter.

Eight Liturgies on Community—one following another from fall until Christmas, and one at Easter.

COMMUNITY LITURGY I

Theme:

Community—Friends Sharing

Symbol:

Rock

Materials Needed:

Toothpicks or craft sticks to build two houses. A tray containing a rock on which one of the houses will stand; and sand on which the other house will stand. Each child will need a special rock to bring at the Offering.

Preparation:

1) Primary Preparation:
The children should construct two toothpick houses beforehand—one on rock, the other on sand. During the liturgy the homilist will pour water on both to demonstrate the Gospel. This will need to be experimented with in advance by the planner in order to make certain that it is the house on sand that will, in fact, collapse. (This advice is the result of experience.)

2) Other Suggestions:
The children should be given as many experiences of rock as possible. It would be good to go on a field trip to collect rocks. Perhaps the children could be taken to a rock show or rock shop. Many rock enthusiasts have small rock polishers of their own and would be willing to lend theirs to your class in addition to demonstrating its use and speaking of their own rock collection. It would be good to "adopt" a very special classroom rock to be kept on the bible table and used in prayer services in the same way as a candle is used. There are many scientific books and filmstrips available on rocks.

3) Reflection:
(for planner and children)
A rock is strong and firm. Picking our way along the rocks when wading, our feet search for the hard, solid feel of rock. When hiking, we like to sit and rest on a solid rock. My friend is like a rock. When I feel uncertain about myself or an idea I have, I tell her. I feel for her opinion the way my feet feel for solid rock in the water. One summer I was very depressed and I was afraid that my feelings would sweep me off my feet, like a strong current in the water. So I called my rock every day, or some days she would call me—just to talk for a couple of minutes. I would tell her in one short sentence how I felt. Once she knew, I knew that I was safe. Sometimes I just like to come and rest on my friend. She's such a good rock. She's always there—no matter what. She's my very own special rock. God gave her to me. She's glad I found her. She was there in the water all along, with the sun shining on her, making her sparkle. But it took a long time until I knew she was my rock. She's a good rock. She's a lot of people's rock. Rocks are meant to be shared. There have been other rocks at other times and other places in my life. When you have to leave a place or a time in your life, you sometimes have to leave your rocks behind for someone else to come and find, but you always take with you the strength that the rock gave you. That strength is a part of you forever. God is a rock to us.

THE LITURGY

Opening Song:

"Alive, Alive"[1]
In the opening song of this liturgy we ask all of our brothers and sisters to take our hands and be our friends.

Greeting:

The celebrant welcomes the children as the very rocks that form the Church.

Penitential Rite:

For the times we have not been friendly to other people. . .

For the times we did not show our love for others. . .

For the times we were not thankful for your gifts. . .

Response:

Jesus, we are sorry.
For the Penitential Rite the children are seated comfortably and informally in a close group on the floor. The leader asks the children to close their eyes, bow their heads, and join hands with one another. The leader will read the Penitential Rite, asking the children to respond. (It would be better if the children, as a group, composed their own Penitential Rite and read it themselves.) Then the leader will invite the children to think of a time when they were not friendly to other people or would not share with other people. If the children wish, they may express this aloud, with all the children responding.

Prayer:

Dear God, we love you very, very much. We know that you love all of us because you are the Father of everybody. Please help us to be kind to other people all the time. We ask. . .

Scripture Reading:

I Peter 2:4-10 (adapted)
Jesus is the living stone. Men threw him away but God chose him and he is precious to God. Set yourselves close to him so that you too may be living stones making a spiritual house. You are a specially chosen people, a people set apart to sing the praises of God who called you out of darkness into his wonderful light. You are the people of God; you have been given his friendship.

In the first scripture reading we are told that we have been chosen by God to be his special friends, the rocks upon which he can build his living house.

Additional Reading:

The Magic Friendmaker[2]
In the additional reading, we discover with Beth the magic of friend-making—sharing!

Response:

Psalm 138:1 (adapted; to the tune of "The Rock Holler")[3]

How good it is; yes, Amen!

To play together; yes, Amen!

Yes, Amen, Amen, Amen!

Gospel Acclamation:

"*Alle, Alle*"[4]

Gospel:

Matthew 7:24-27
See also: *The House on the Rock* (Matthew 7:24-27)[5]
(Demonstration can be done during the Gospel or the Homily.)

In the gospel Jesus shows us the importance of building our friendships on true faith and true love.

Homily:

Suggestion:

When Beth saw Jean sitting alone on the step, how do you think she felt and what did she think? (Bring out the faith she placed in Jean.) What made Beth believe in Jean? (Her smile.) Did Jean believe in Beth? (If Jean had not believed in Beth she would not have smiled.) Was the rock really magic? Does everybody need a friend? Is it hard to make friends? What does this mean: "If you want to have a friend, you have to be one yourself"? What is a friend like? Talk about the two houses in the gospel and demonstrate with the houses made by the children.

Is God a special friend to you? What do you need to be a special friend of God? Like Jean, God is always sitting and smiling, and waiting for you. Is God a *best* friend? Do you talk to him? Do you do things with him? How can you tell God that you want to be *best* friends?

Prayer of the Faithful:

For all the people in the world who have no friends. . .

So that we will always be best friends with God. . .

So that we will always be good to our friends. . .

68

Response:

Lord, hear our prayer.
(The children should be invited to add their own petitions.)

Offering:

Each child will bring his special rock as a sign of his friendship with God.

Offertory Song:

(to the tune of "The Rock Holler")

The Lord's our rock; yes, Amen!
The Lord's our friend; yes, Amen!
Yes, Amen, Amen, Amen!

We bring rocks; yes, Amen!
To show our love; yes, Amen!
Yes, Amen, Amen, Amen!

Lord, make us strong; yes, Amen!
As strong as rocks; yes, Amen!
Yes, Amen, Amen, Amen!

Prayer Over the Gifts:

Lord, please take our water and wine, our bread and our rocks as a sign that we want to be your friend and we want you to be our friend. We ask. . .

Preface:

(Use simplest one possible.)

Holy, Holy, Holy:

(sung, if possible)[6]

Acclamation:

(Sing "Christ Has Died.")[7]

Amen:

(sung—The children might be invited to clap their hands in applause.)

Our Father:

(Join hands and recite.)

Rite of Peace:

Each child gives his rock to another child with an appropriate greeting such as, "I want to be your friend."

Communion:

(under both species, if possible)

Communion Song:

(to the tune of "The Rock Holler")

Jesus came; yes, Amen!
Upon this earth; yes, Amen!
Yes, Amen, Amen, Amen!

For many years; yes, Amen!
He played among men; yes, Amen!
Yes, Amen, Amen, Amen!

But he had to leave; yes, Amen!
To go to the Father; yes, Amen!
Yes, Amen, Amen, Amen!

He gave us a sign; yes, Amen!
A sign of love; yes, Amen!
Yes, Amen, Amen, Amen!

His body and blood; yes, Amen!
To be with us; yes, Amen!
Yes, Amen, Amen, Amen!

A community; yes, Amen!
Built upon rock; yes, Amen!
Yes, Amen, Amen, Amen!

Thanksgiving:

The children sit in a circle with heads bowed in silent prayer. The leader, in a very soft, reverent, gentle, and intense voice sets an atmosphere of wonder and awe as he (or she) invites each child to say a prayer either silently or aloud as he holds the rock which is passed around the circle.

Prayer:

Dear God, thank you for loving us so much. Please help us to learn to love as you loved. We ask. . .

Blessing:

Suggestions:

May God always be your joy and your strength;
And may you always feel that he is your personal friend.

May you always share the love of God with others;
And may you rest in the strength of his love.

And may God bless you in the name of the Father, and of the Son, and of the Holy Spirit.

Closing Song:

(to the tune of "The Rock Holler")

It's up to us; yes, Amen!
To go out today; yes, Amen!
Yes, Amen, Amen, Amen!

To be signs of love; yes, Amen!
To one another; yes, Amen!
Yes, Amen, Amen, Amen!

Christ is with us; yes, Amen!
When we love; yes, Amen!
Yes, Amen, Amen, Amen!

We are rocks; yes, Amen!
To one another, yes, Amen!
Yes, Amen, Amen, Amen!

Treats:

Candy rocks (These can usually be purchased in a grocery store.)

References

1. "Alive, Alive," Album #2, *Life, Love, Joy,* Silver Burdett, General Learning Corporation, Morristown, New Jersey 07960.

2. *The Magic Friendmaker,* Gladys Baker Bond, Whitman Publishing Co., Racine, Wisconsin.

3. "The Rock Holler," *Run, Come See* Album, Robert Blue, F.E.L. Publications, Ltd., 1925 Pontius Avenue, Los Angeles, California 90025.

4. "Alle, Alle," Miffleton, World Library Publications, Inc., 2145 Central Parkway, Cincinnati, Ohio 45214.

5. *The House on the Rock,* Jane R. Latourette, Arch Books, Concordia Publishing House, 3558 Jefferson Avenue, St. Louis, Missouri 63118.

6. "Holy, Holy, Holy," *Welcome In* Album, Joe Wise, ASCAP; North American Liturgy Resources, 300 East McMillan Street, Cincinnati, Ohio 45219.

7. "Christ Has Died," *A New Day* Album, Joe Wise, World Library of Sacred Music, 2145 Central Parkway, Cincinnati, Ohio 45214.

COMMUNITY LITURGY II

Theme:

Community—Families Giving

Symbol:

Tree

Materials Needed:

Materials for story of *The Giving Tree*
This liturgy suggests that at the Offering, each child will bring some gift for someone in his family. It might be good to have the children make place mats for their family to use at dinner, or decorate paper napkins, or napkin rings, or make nut cups, or place cards. The materials needed will depend then upon the project chosen.

Popcorn (enough for one popcorn ball for each child to be used as the top part of a tree).

Tootsie Rolls (one for each child to be used as the tree trunk).

Red hots (to be used as apples on the tree).

Green food coloring (a few drops to be added to the syrup).

Syrup for popcorn balls.

Recipe for popcorn ball syrup (enough for 2½ qts. popcorn):

¾ cup light corn syrup

1½ cup sugar

½ cup water

¼ tsp. salt

Combine the above ingredients in a heavy saucepan. Bring to a boil and continue cooking until syrup reaches the hard ball stage. Stir occasionally. Add food coloring and pour over popcorn. Stir quickly and form balls quickly as the syrup hardens rapidly. Grease hands to form balls. Add red hots on outside.

Make trees by attaching Tootsie Rolls to popcorn balls.

Preparation:

1) *Primary Preparation:*
The community should gather around a small tree (or large branch). Talk with the children about how a tree is like a family. Decide what kind of gifts you would like to make for your family. These are given in the Offering of the Mass. You may prefer to present pictures of

thoughtful things you will do for your family; e.g., tending younger brothers and sisters while mother is getting dinner.

Make the popcorn balls. (Caution: This takes quick hands while the syrup is still hot. It might not be a good idea to plan to involve the children.)

2) *Other Suggestions:*
The tree used for this liturgy should be used as the center of many subsequent classes and class activities and should be adopted as the "community tree." It can be decorated to carry out the theme of subsequent liturgies and can be used to ornament the celebration room.

You may want to read for the children about family customs in other lands. It would be good to take the children for a walk in the forest so they can experience together the hugeness, the strength, and the cry of the trees to "life up your hearts!"

If it is fall and the leaves are changing, then make much of the beauty of trees.

Reflection: (for planner)

Thomas Merton says that a tree gives glory to God first of all by being a tree. We give comfort to our family first of all by being who we really are, by being part of the family, by truly being one with the other members. Our interdependence ought to make one another feel valuable. We must need our families. We must recognize and express the need we have to be brother or sister, to be needed because we are brother or sister.

THE LITURGY

Opening Song:

"Alive, Alive" (chorus and verse 3)[1]
In the opening song of this liturgy we sing about our homes—the place where, all together, we grow in learning how to give.

Greeting:

The celebrant welcomes the children as branches of different trees, all making up God's forest.

Penitential Rite:

For the times we do not help our mothers . . .
For the times we do not obey our dads . . .
For the times we fight with our brothers and sisters . . .

Response:

Jesus, we are sorry.
For the Penitential Rite the children are seated comfortably and informally in a close group on the floor. The leader asks the children to close their eyes, bow their heads, and join hands with one another. The leader will read the Penitential Rite, asking the children to respond. (It would be better if the children, as a group, composed their own Penitential Rite and read it themselves.) Then the leader will invite the children to think of a time when they did not give to someone in their family. If the children wish, they may express this aloud with all the children responding.

Prayer:

Dear God, please help us to understand what it means to be one with the other people in my family. Help me to give myself to the other people in my family. We ask . . .

Scripture Reading:

1 John 4:7-16 (adapted)
My dear children,
let us love one another
since love comes from God
and everyone who loves is a child of God and knows God.
Anyone who does not love can never have known God,
because God is love.
God's love for us was shown
when God sent into the world his only Son
so that we could have life through him;
this is the love I mean;
not our love for God,
but God's love for us when he sent his Son
to take our sins away.
My dear people,
since God has loved us so much,
we too should love one another.
No one has ever seen God;
but as long as we love one another
God will live in us.
and his love will be complete in us.
We can know that we are living in him
and he is living in us
because he lets us share his Spirit.
We ourselves saw and we testify
that the Father sent his Son
as savior of the world.

If anyone acknowledges that Jesus is the Son of God,
God lives in him, and he lives in God.
We ourselves have known and believe in
God's love for us.
God is love
and anyone who lives in love lives in God,
and God lives in him.

Additional Reading:

Have two children pantomime *The Giving Tree*[2] while the other children recite the story in choral speaking.

In the additional reading we see that complete happiness is in giving—in giving everything, all of our life.

Response:

"She's Just an Old Stump"[3]

Gospel Acclamation:

"Alle, Alle"

Gospel:

Luke 2:39-52
In the gospel we see how difficult it is to recognize and understand the operation of God in those closest to us, our families.

Homily:

Suggestion:

Small children experience many conflicts with their parents and with their brothers and sisters. They do not understand the cause and the nature of these conflicts. Often children feel guilty and blame themselves for upsets between their parents. Many times children keep feelings of inferiority concealed within themselves. In today's gospel, Jesus did not apologize to his parents and keep the real reason for his conduct from them. He simply explained the problem. Perhaps neither Jesus nor his parents understood. Here is an opportunity to show even small children that giving in a family means not only doing things for others but trying to understand, accepting what cannot be understood without blaming anyone, accepting ourselves and explaining our feelings and trusting the acceptance of the others in the family.

Prayer of the Faithful:

For all the families in the world . . .
So that we will grow in loving and giving . . .
So that we will not be selfish . . .

Response:

Lord, hear our prayer.
(The children should be invited to add their own petitions.)

Offering:

Each child brings what he made for his family or a picture of what he will do for someone in the family.

Offertory Song:

"Tree Song"[4]

Prayer Over the Gifts:

Lord, please accept our gifts as a sign that we give ourselves to you constantly as we give ourselves to those you have placed so close to us—our families.

Preface:

God, you are the Father of all of us. We all belong to your family. We should praise you and thank you all the time because you gave us Jesus to be our brother. With everybody in the whole human family we say:

Holy, Holy, Holy:

(sung)

Eucharistic Prayer:

#2

Acclamation:

(Sing "Christ Has Died.")

Amen:

(sung)

Our Father:

(Join hands and recite.)

Rite of Peace:

An appropriate wish would be: May you be a Giving Tree!

Communion:

(under both species, if possible)

Communion Song:

"Thank You Hymn"[5]

Thanksgiving:

The children sit in a circle with heads bowed in silent prayer. The leader, in a very soft, reverent, gentle and intense voice sets an atmosphere of wonder and awe as he (or she) invites each child to say a prayer either silently or aloud thanking God for each member of his family.

Prayer:

Dear God, thank you for making me part of a family. Thank you for giving us Jesus to be part of the human family and for showing us how to love in a family.

Blessing:

Suggestion:

May your family bless you,
And may you be a blessing to your family.

May you treasure one another in your hearts,
And may you seek to understand one another's ways.

May you always grow in wisdom and age and grace,
Before God and man.

And may God bless you in the name of the Father, and
of the Son, and of the Holy Spirit.

Closing Song:

"Come, Go and Climb a Tree"[6]

Treats:

A Giving Tree made of green popcorn balls, Tootsie Roll trunk, red hots for apples, and the message—"Be a Giving Tree!"

References

1. "Alive, Alive," album #2, *Life, Love, Joy,* Silver Burdett, General Learning Corporation, Morristown, New Jersey 07960.
2. *The Giving Tree,* Shel Silverstein, Harper & Row Publishers, New York 10022.
3. "She's Just an Old Stump," *Come Out!* album, Jack Miffleton, World Library Publications, 2145 Central Parkway, Cincinnati, Ohio 45214.
4. "Tree Song," *Run, Come See* album, Robert Blue, F.E.L. Publications, Ltd., 1925 Pontius Avenue, Los Angeles, California 90025.
5. "Thank You Hymn," *Run, Come See,* Robert Blue, F.E.L. Publications, Ltd., 1925 Pontius Avenue, Los Angeles, California 90025.
6. "Come, Go and Climb a Tree," *Up With People,* Moral Re-Armament, Inc., 833 South Flower Street, Los Angeles, California 90017.

COMMUNITY LITURGY III

Theme:

Community—World Interdependence

Symbol:

Island

Materials Needed:

Materials to make a flower favor to be presented at the Offering and later to be given to someone such as an elderly person.

Your own creativity may suggest very ornate flowers; or, your flowers could simply be construction paper posies with mint patty centers. You may wish to add pipe cleaner stems and construction paper leaves; and pot it in a small margarine or cottage cheese container. It would be good if each child would attach a small greeting card to his flower.

If the project suggested below is used, each child will need one small, relatively shallow dish (such as a meat pie container), a piece of clay, toothpicks, pebbles, and scraps of construction paper.

Preparation:

1) *Primary Preparation Before the Liturgy:*

Each child could be given a small container such as a meat pie tin and a piece of clay. The clay could be pressed into the bottom of the container and "mountains" could be formed. Water can then be added to the dish so that only the clay "mountains" are visible, representing "islands." The children may want to give their islands names such as "Fatherland," "Brotherhood," "Loveland," "Friendship," etc. Symbolic flags could be made from construction paper and toothpicks and mounted on the islands. Each child should be invited to give the class a guided tour of his own "small world," explaining the reasons for the names of the different lands and the symbolism of the flags. Tiny trees, rocks, animals, and other decorations may be added. The water that touches and surrounds all of the "lands" could be symbolic of the presence of God to all people and lands. (This concept could be related to Liturgy I, Part I—water.)

Prepare the choral reading for the Thanksgiving in the liturgy.

2) *Other Suggestions:*
Take the children for a walk on the shore of a lake or the bank of a stream. Have the children watch for "islands" and observe the land that connects them to other land. If possible, have the children work together to build a small island in the shallow water.

3) *Reflection:* (for planner)

Globs of isolated protoplasm
                         spiritized . . .
Reaching out—
In limitless water . . .
          Reaching out—
Amoeba-like . . .
               Reaching out—
For an indefinable God . . .
                    Reaching out—
     Full of laughter . . .
Reaching out—
          Full of tears . . .
               Reaching out—
                    Full of hopes . . .
                    Reaching out—
                         Full of fears . . .
                         Reaching out—
     All . . .
     Reaching out—
TOGETHER!

We all experience the same basic needs, the same weaknesses, hungers, doubts, loneliness, and emptiness. Yet these universal experiences are uniquely felt by each individual. Each individual also possesses a special talent for listening, accepting, cheering, understanding, consoling, and forgiving. God called us in our Baptism to share in the priesthood of Jesus; to bring his life to others, to make him present to others, to share him with them—to be "holy communion."

THE LITURGY

Opening Song:

"It's a Small World"[1]
In the opening song of this liturgy we ask everyone to understand that there is just one moon and one golden sun and one smile for friendship in this small world.

Greeting:

The celebrant welcomes the children, asking them to join hands for a minute to become aware that in the liturgy we are all one just as all land is one underneath.

Penitential Rite:

For hurting other people . . .
For taking things from other people . . .
For not paying attention to other people . . .

Response:

Jesus, we are sorry.

For the Penitential Rite the children are seated comfortably and informally in a close group on the floor. The leader asks the children to close their eyes, bow their heads, and join hands with one another. The leader will read the Penitential Rite, asking the children to respond. (It would be better if the children, as a group, composed their own Penitential Rite and read it themselves.) Then the leader will invite the children to think of a time when they were not good to someone. If the children wish, they may express this aloud, with all the children responding.

Prayer:

God, please help us to understand one another, to be kind to one another, to trust one another, and to see the good in one another. We ask this through Jesus Christ . . .

First Scripture Reading:

1 Corinthians 12:12-21, 27 (adapted)
Your body, though it is made up of many different parts, is all just one thing together. So it is with Jesus. We are all baptized in the one Spirit in Jesus. The body is not the same as any one of its parts. If the foot were to say, "I am not a hand and so I do not belong to the body," would that mean that it stopped being part of the body? If the ear were to say, "I am not an eye, and so I do not belong to the body," would that mean that it was not part of the body? If your whole body was just one eye, how would you hear anything? If it was just one ear, how would you smell anything?

Instead of that, God put all the separate parts into the body on purpose. If all the parts were the same, how could it be a body? As it is, the parts are many but the body is one. The eye cannot say to the hand, "I do not need you," nor can the head say to the feet, "I do not need you." Now all of you together are Christ's body, but each of you is a different part of it.

In the first scripture reading we see that we are all one person in Jesus, just as all land is one land underneath.

Additional Reading:

The Little Island[2]
In this reading the cat demands that the fish tell him how the island is part of the land. The fish invites the cat to come and see in the deep dark secret places of the sea. But since the cat can't swim he just has to believe the fish when the fish tells him how all land is one land under the sea.

Response:

(to the tune of "This Land Is Your Land"[3])
All land is one land, we are all one man;
We are united in the Holy Spirit.
God is our Father; we are his children.
His love is one in you and me.

All land is one land, we all are one man.
We are united in Jesus Christ.
He is our brother; we share his body.
His love is one in you and me.

Gospel Acclamation:

"Alle, Alle"

Gospel:

Matthew 25:34-41
See also: *The Children's Living Bible*[4] paraphrased
In the gospel Jesus points out that what we do to someone we do to him since we are all one just as land is one land underneath.

Homily:

Suggestion:
Discuss with the children what it means to be all one. Draw from the children a large number of ways in which we can show that we care as much about our neighbor as we do about ourselves. Have the children think of ways in which they can give someone a preference over themselves. This might include such things as letting other members of the family have first choice in T.V. shows, games, food, jobs, etc.

Prayer of the Faithful:

For people who need people . . .
For all the old people . . .
For all the people who do not know that they need other people . . .
For all the people in the world . . .

Response:

Lord, hear our prayer.
(The children should be invited to add their own petitions.)

Offering:

Each child will bring a flower favor. These will be taken with good tidings to the elderly later in the day.

Offertory Song:

"Whatsoever You Do"[5]

Prayer Over the Gifts:

Lord, please take our gifts as we bring them to your lonely people. Take our gifts as we bring them now to you with our water and wine, our bread and our hearts. Please fill these gifts with your presence and love so that the people to whom we bring this liturgy may come to know you better. We ask . . .

Preface:

God, our Father, you made all of us to be separate, and yet all to be one as all land is one underneath. We praise you and thank you because you are so wise and you do everything just right. You even made your Son a human person to be one with all of us. With all of the people in the whole world we say:

Holy, Holy, Holy:

(sung)

Eucharistic Prayer:

#2

Acclamation:

Sing "Christ Has Died"

Amen:

(Sung. The children might be invited to clap their hands in applause.)

Our Father:

(Join hands and recite.)

Rite of Peace:

An appropriate greeting might be: "I want to be one with you." Or— "I need you."

Communion:

(under both species, if possible)

Communion Song:

"Community Song"[6]

Thanksgiving:

Choral recitation—
We are all different.
We feel differently.
We think differently.
We all look different.
We all talk and walk differently.
Each one of us has to make up his own mind about things.
But underneath we are all one.
We all belong to one another.
We are a community.

Prayer:

God, thank you for coming with us and making us all one in you, and in Jesus our brother in whom we pray.

Blessing:

May you know in your heart that we are all one;
And may your eyes shine with the secret of it.
May you know your need for others;
And give to others what they need.
May you open your hearts to the deep secrets hidden in others;
And may you open to others the deep secrets of your own heart.
And may God bless you in the name of the Father,
And of the Son, and of the Holy Spirit.

Closing Song:

"Up With People"[7]

References

1. *It's a Small World,* Disneyland Records, 477 Madison Avenue, New York, New York 10022.

2. *The Little Island,* Golden MacDonald, Doubleday & Co., Inc., 277 Park Avenue, Garden City, New York 10017.

3. "This Land Is Your Land," Woody Guthrie, Ludlow Music, Inc., 10 Columbus Circle, New York, New York 10019.

4. *The Children's Living Bible,* Tyndale House Publishers, 336 Gunderson Drive, Wheaton, Illinois 60187.

5. "Whatsoever You Do," Rev. W. F. Jabusch, ACTA Foundation, 4848 N. Clark Street, Chicago, Illinois 60640.

6. "Community Song," *Run, Come See,* Robert Blue, F.E.L. Publications, Ltd., 1925 Pontius Avenue, Los Angeles, California 90025.

7. *Up With People,* Moral Re-Armament, Inc., 833 South Flower Street, Los Angeles, California 90017.

COMMUNITY LITURGY IV

Theme:

Community—Self-understanding

Symbol:

Jack-O'-Lantern

Materials Needed:

A large pumpkin, a candle, a knife and some spoons for a jack-o'-lantern. A paper plate for each child to make a mask. A piece of yarn for each child to fasten the mask on his head. Some scraps of colored construction paper for masks (eyes, hair, etc.).

Preparation:

1) *Primary Preparation:*
   The community should gather around a large pumpkin. Each child should have an opportunity to handle it. In this way the pumpkin will become part of him and he will more strongly identify with its meaning. After a spontaneous discussion about pumpkins and Halloween, the top will be cut from the pumpkin. Each child will smell the pumpkin and react. Let each child share in removing the seeds from the pumpkin. Many children like to feel the slimy seeds and surrounding pulp. Encourage the children to handle the seeds. *It is important to save these seeds* for a special project in the spring.

   After talking about masks with the children give each child a paper plate and some colored scraps to make a mask. Fasten a piece of yarn on each side of the mask to be tied behind the child's head.

2) *Other Suggestions:*
   If you have celebrated the Tree Liturgy with the children and have kept your tree, you could invite the children to make Halloween decorations for the tree. The children will enjoy making large self-portraits to be hung in the celebration room. You might ask the children to write stories or make booklets about themselves describing themselves— their appearance, their feelings, their likes and dislikes, what they like best about themselves, what they like least about themselves, what they think is funny about themselves.

3) *Reflection:*
   (for planner and children)
   Who do you say I am?
   Who do I say that I am?
   When will I know who I am?
   How far is it to who I am?

Am I who I say I am?
How can I know if I am true to myself?
How can I tell you who I am?
Who wants to know who I am?
Who do I say other people are?
Do I know who other people are?
Masks are hard to see through.
At first they are awkward.
But they sort of grow on after a while.
I really don't know that I'm wearing one.
It takes a friend to see through that, I guess.
Oh well, they didn't know who Jesus was either.
Did you, Jesus?
Who do you say that I am?

THE LITURGY

Opening Song:

"God Made Us All"[1]
In the opening song of the liturgy we recall that God made each of us in his own special way—unique, yet all children of God. Children will walk in with masks, someone will carry a lighted jack-o'-lantern.

Greeting:

The celebrant welcomes the children as God's very special jack-o'-lanterns. Each child has a special face carved by God and the light of God shines out from each of them as the light shines from the jack-o'-lantern.

Penitential Rite:

For the times we are not truthful . . .
For the times we do not see the good in other people . . .
For the times we do not use the gifts God has given us . . .

Response:

Jesus, we are sorry.
For the Penitential Rite the children are seated comfortably and informally in a close group on the floor. The leaders ask the children to close their eyes, bow their heads, and join hands with one another. The leader will read the Penitential Rite, asking the children to respond. (It would be better if the children, as a group, composed their own Penitential Rite and read it themselves.) Then the leader will invite the children to think of a time when they were not truthful. If the children wish, they may express this aloud, with all the children responding.

Prayer:

Dear Lord, let the people who have masks on take them off. Make us not have to wear masks again. Help us to be helpful friends to those who wear masks. We ask . . .

Scripture Reading:

Colossians 3:1-4 (adapted)
"Since you have been brought to true life with Jesus, you must look for the true and the good things in life. Let your thoughts be on the things of God, for your true life is hidden with Jesus in God. But when Jesus is shown forth—and he is your real life—you will be shown forth too in all your glory with him."

(A jack-o'-lantern is dead and not much of a jack-o'-lantern at all unless we put a light in it. The scripture reading tells us that we are dead and not persons at all unless we have the light of Jesus in us. He is a true light which we do not see because he is hidden in God.)

Additional Reading:

Who Are You?[2]
In the additional reading we think about the many ways in which we are all very different. We realize that only we can be ourselves.

Response:

Psalm 139 (adapted)[3]
God sees us and knows us.
Father, you see me and know me when I fail to understand.
God sees us and knows us.
You know if I am sitting or standing; you read my thoughts.
God sees us and knows us.
You know if I walk or lie down; you know everything.
God sees us and knows us.
Before I say a word you know all about it.
God sees us and knows us.
You know me through and through.
God sees us and knows us.

This response could be done as a choral reading with two choruses alternating, or you might have one child read the first line, all respond, another child read the second line, all respond, etc.

Gospel Acclamation:

"Alle, Alle"

Gospel:

Luke 9:18-20

Homily:

Suggestion:

God understands us. He knows just what we are like—how we think and how we feel. Our thoughts and our feelings are always good and beautiful when we are filled with the light of his love. God wants us to share our thoughts and feelings with others. He wants this life that is hidden in us to shine out—to warm and cheer other people. He wants other people to see and to understand this light that is hidden in us. God wants other people to see who we really are.

Then other people can help us to know ourselves and to understand who we really are deep inside.

Prayer of the Faithful:

For the people who do not understand other people . . .
For the people who do not understand themselves . . .
For the people who feel that other people do not understand them . . .

Response:

Lord, hear our prayer.
(The children should be invited to add their own petitions.)

Offering:

Each child comes in procession to the altar wearing his mask. He takes it off and gives it to the celebrant as a sign of his wanting to be his real self and to give his real self to God and to other people. Celebrant puts masks on side table.

Offertory Song:

(to the tune of "Ray, the Rangy Rhino")[4]
Who am I? What am I? Can anybody tell?
Oh, I'm me (name). God knows me very well.

Prayer Over the Gifts:

Bless the masks, the bread, the water, and the wine. These gifts are our sign that we want to belong to you. Please help us always to be true to the persons you are calling us to be. We ask. . .

Preface:

Celebrant's choice

Holy, Holy, Holy:

(sung)

Eucharistic Prayer:

(Choose the one the children relate to best.)

Acclamation:

Sing "Christ Has Died."

Amen:

(Sing. The children might be invited to clap their hands in applause.)

Our Father:

(Join hands and recite.)

Rite of Peace:

Each child shakes hands with all of the other children and says: Be yourself!

Communion:

(under both species, if possible)

Communion Song:

"Everything Is Beautiful"[5]

Thanksgiving:

The children sit in a circle, with heads bowed in silent prayer. The jack-o'-lantern is in the center of the circle. The leader, in a very soft, reverent, gentle, and intense voice sets an atmosphere of wonder and awe as he (or she) invites each child to say a prayer either silently or aloud as he holds the jack-o'-lantern which is passed around the circle.

Prayer:

God, thank you for making us all in your own special way. Help us to remember always that the one you love is our true self. We ask. . .

Blessing:

May God fill you with his light;
Any may your whole being shine forth his presence.

May you always be happy to be who you are;
And may you help other people to be happy to be who they are.

And may God bless you in the name of the Father,
And of the Son, and of the Holy Spirit.

Closing Song:

"Halloween Song"[6]

References:

1. "God Made Us All," *Come Out!* Jack Miffleton, World Library Publications, Inc., 2145 Central Parkway, Cincinnati, Ohio 45214.

2. *Who Are You?* Joan and Roger Bradfield, Whitman Publication Co., Racine, Wisconsin.

3. *Come Out!* celebration booklet, World Library Publications, Inc., 2145 Central Parkway, Cincinnati, Ohio 45214.

4. *Come Out!* celebration booket, World Library Publications, Inc., 2145 Central Parkway, Cincinnati, Ohio 45214.

5. *Everything Is Beautiful,* Ray Stevens, Barnaby Records, 816 North Lacienda Boulevard, Los Angeles, California 90069.

6. "Halloween Song," *Come Out!* Neil Blunt, World Library Publications, Inc., 2145 Central Parkway, Cincinnati, Ohio 45214.

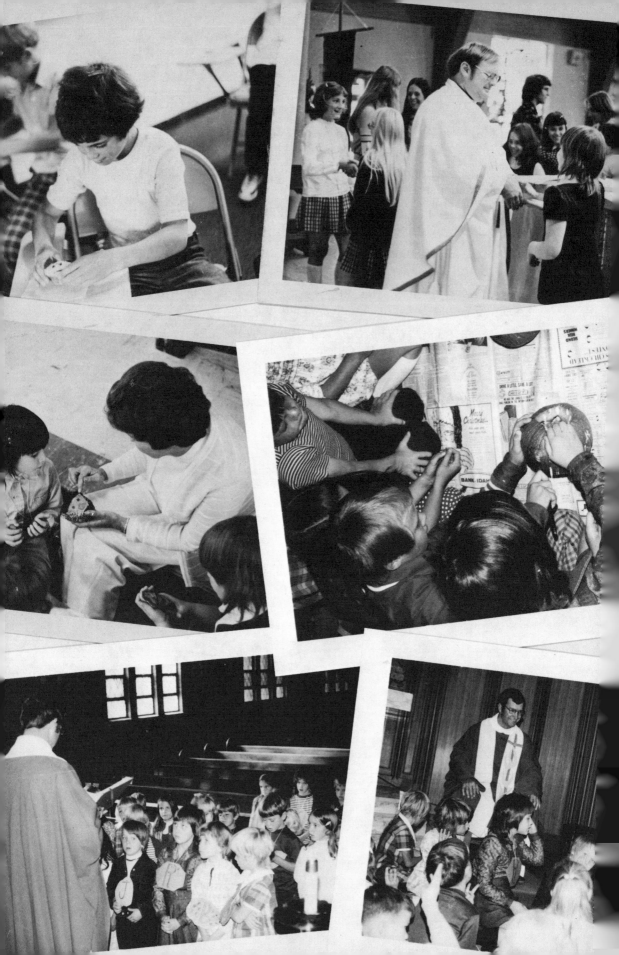

COMMUNITY LITURGY V

Theme:

Community—Thanksgiving

Symbol:

Table, bread

Materials Needed:

If the children make the paten and/or chalice, someone who works in ceramics will need to be consulted well in advance to arrange all the materials.

Material for the altar cloth (this depends upon the table being used).

Freehand painting by the children on the altar cloth is ideal but it might be simpler to get a piece of felt or construction paper for each child to cut out a design that can be attached to the altar cloth. If each child has a small photo of himself, he could cut it out and attach it to his design.

One excellent project would be for the children to make the altar breads. There are many good recipes available, any of which could be used.

If the projects suggested below are used, construction paper will be needed for the pilgrim hats. Materials such as burlap and felt will be needed for the banners; or poster paper, magazine pictures, or other paper if a collage is made. Newspaper, wheat paste, Elmer's glue, and tempera paint will be needed if papier-mache is made for tree decorations.

Preparation:

1) *Primary Preparation Before the Liturgy:*
Any experience of bread baking, breaking, and sharing with the children would be good along with the natural dialogue that would accompany the event. Children love homemade breads fresh from the oven with honey butter. It would be good to precede this bread-baking experience with the Arch Book story: *The Fisherman's Surprise!*[1] Discuss with the children what Jesus meant when he told the apostles to feed his sheep; and how we can feed his sheep. Listen prayerfully to the song, "Do You Really Love Me?"[2] from the *Hi, God* album. The children might enjoy singing this song while waiting for the breads to bake. Pilgrim hats are easy for the children to construct and children enjoy wearing them. The following illustrations may be helpful:

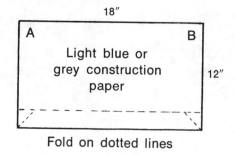

18″

A   B

Light blue or
grey construction   12″
paper

Fold on dotted lines

GIRL'S HAT
Overlap corners A and B
and staple. The girls enjoy
decorating these hats.

Front View   Back View

BOY'S HAT
Overlap sides A and B and
staple. Take a 9″ x 12″
sheet of black construction
paper and cut it into an
oblong shape. Cut a hole
(approximately 5½″ in di-
ameter) in the center of the
oblong piece. Paste tabs
of side C on the bottom
side of the oblong (brim)
piece.

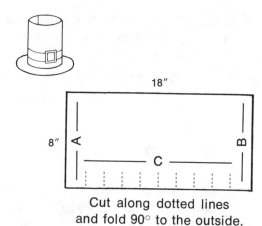

18″

8″ A   C   B

Cut along dotted lines
and fold 90° to the outside.

The children might like to decorate the Giving Tree with things for which
they are especially grateful. These may be freehand cutouts, magazine pictures, or papier-mache. To make papier-mache decorations,
form the desired objects from crushed newspaper. Wrap several layers
of newspaper strips coated with papier-mache around the object. Allow
the object to dry, then paint it. Papier-mache paste can be made from
wheat paste (purchased in a paint shop) and water mixed to right consistency. A small amount of Elmer's glue could be added, but it is not
necessary. It would be good to have the children make a thank-you
banner or collage.

The children should compose their own thanksgiving litany to be used
in the Thanksgiving at the liturgy. An account of the first American
Thanksgiving should be composed by the children, to be used as the
additional reading at the liturgy.

2) *Reflection:*
(for planner and children)
America is a land of all kinds of people of different countries, different
languages, and different customs; but on Thanksgiving Day all the

members of a family of whatever ethnic group try to get to their own homes to eat together at the same table a very special meal. Sharing a meal together is symbolic of sharing life. It reminds us that heaven is a kingdom of all kinds of people, all sharing the food of love and understanding at the table of Christ, the life. At the Mass, all kinds of people come together to partake of the one body, Christ—forgiving, understanding, listening, sharing, giving, loving—all at the table of the Lord.

Jesus once ate supper with sinners and publicans. He knew that they were sinners, yet he wanted very much to eat with them because he had come to call, not the just, but sinners, to his banqueting table. Each time I come to the supper, I know that I am indeed called. The priest holds in his hands the very person, Jesus. He says to me, This is Jesus who takes away the sin (the hunger and emptiness) of the world: happy are those called to his supper. Each time I eat at this supper, I become more identified as a sinner; and each time my hunger increases, yet each time I am more filled with Jesus. The more we recognize our need, the more we receive—the greater becomes our participation in the Thanksgiving.

THE LITURGY

Opening Song:

"We All Stand at Your Table"[3]
In the opening song of this liturgy, we stand before God—as we are, poor and hungry. We see that we are all one in our poverty. We are all the same—sinners, poor and hungry, all needing our daily bread.

Greeting:

The celebrant, in the place of Jesus, welcomes the children whole-heartedly, inviting them to come even closer around the table of the Lord that they may be filled to overflowing with the word and presence of Jesus.

Penitential Rite:

For the times I did not share the gifts God gave me. . .

For the times I did not help my mother set the table. . .

For the times I have not been thankful to God and other people. . .

Response:

Jesus, we are sorry.
For the Penitential Rite the children are seated comfortably and in-formally in a close group on the floor. The leader asks the children to

close their eyes, bow their heads, and join hands with one another. The leader will read the Penitential Rite, asking the children to respond. (It would be better if the children, as a group, composed their own Penitential Rite and read it themselves.) Then the leader will invite the children to think of a time when they were not thankful for God's gifts. If the children wish, they may express this aloud, with all the children responding.

Prayer:

Dear God, thank you for the thanks that other people give us. . .

Thank you most of all for giving us the Mass. . . . We pray this through. . .

First Scripture Reading:

Psalm 67 (adapted)
May God show kindness and bless us,
And make his face smile on us!
For then the earth will recognize your way,
and all the nations will know of your power to save.

Let the nations praise you, O God,
let all the nations praise you!

Let the nations shout and sing for joy
since you are true and fair to the world;
You give to all the people what is fair,
on earth you rule the nations.

Let the nations praise you God;
let all the nations praise you!

The soil has given its harvest,
God, our God, has blessed us.
May God bless us, and let him be served
to the very ends of the earth.

In the first scripture reading we call on all the nations of the earth to praise God. We recognize that not just our own country but all nations are God's country, land on which the face of God smiles.

Additional Reading:

A short summary, drawn up by the group, of the first American Thanksgiving.

In the additional reading we see how truly dependent upon God the pilgrims felt. We share their deep feeling of gratitude.

Response and Gospel

Acclamation:

(takeoff on the song, "Sons of God"[4])
Sons of God, hear his holy word;
Gather 'round the table of the Lord.
See his actions; hear his words;
And we'll sing a song of love
Allelu, Allelu, Allelu, Alleluia!

Gospel:

Luke 22:7-20 (adapted)
In this Gospel, Jesus uses food and drink to show
how much he wants to be with us.
"The feast of the Passover was coming!"
Jesus said to Peter and John, "Go and get things
ready for the Passover feast."
"Where do you want us to prepare it?" they asked.

"Go into the city," Jesus said. "There you will meet a man carrying a
pitcher of water. Follow him into the house he enters and say to him,
'The Master says for you to show us the room for our Passover feast.'
He will show you a large room upstairs all ready for us. Go ahead and
get the meal ready there."

So they went off to the city and found everything just as Jesus had said.
Then they prepared the meal there.

When it was time for dinner, Jesus said, "I have looked forward to this
meal anxiously. I have wanted so much to eat with you before I suffer."
Then Jesus took a cup of wine into his hands. He gave thanks to God.
He said, "Take this and share it among you. This cup is a promise of
friendship and oneness in my blood, which will be poured out for you.
I shall not drink wine again until I drink with you in the kingdom of God."

Homily:

Suggestion:

Dialogue with the children on the great love of Jesus and his tremendous desire to be with us. Lead the children to have a feeling for his
presence and love in other people and help them to want to give his
presence and love to others—to *be* the bread of Jesus to others.

Prayer of the Faithful:

For all the old people. . .
For all the sick people. . .
For all the people who have died. . .
For all the sad people. . .
For all the hungry people. . .

Response:

Father, hear our prayer.
(The children should be invited to add their own petitions.)

Offering:

The children will bring tablecloth, chalice, paten and breads which they made themselves.

Offertory Song:

"Take Our Bread"[5]

Prayer Over the Gifts:

Lord, please accept the gifts we prepared for your holy meal and unite all of us in the one meal with Jesus our brother.

Preface:

God, you are so good! You love us and give us everything that is good. We should praise you and thank you all the time. Best of all, you gave us your only Son, Jesus, to be our bread. With all the good and beautiful and strong things in the whole world we say:

Holy, Holy, Holy:

(sung)

Eucharistic Prayer:

(Choose the one the children relate to best.)

Acclamation:

(Sing "Lord, By Your Cross")[6]

Amen:

(Sung—The children might be invited to clap their hands in applause.)

Our Father:

(Join hands and recite.)

Rite of Peace:

An appropriate greeting would be: "Be the bread of Jesus"; or, "Thank you for being you."

Communion:

(under both species, if possible)

Communion Song:

"We All Stand at Your Table" (Dance as for the Virginia Reel.)

Alternative: Silently listen to the song, "We Are Your Bread."

Thanksgiving:

For our families and relatives. . .
For our friends. . .
For our food. . .
For our houses. . .
For our clothes. . .
For the trees and hills. . .
For the Church and the priests. . .
For all the people in the world. . .
For all your love. . .

Response:

Thank you, God.

Prayer:

Dear God, we have a lot of fun at dinner. We like to share food and laughter, and talk at our dinner table. Help us always to share whatever we have; we pray in Jesus' name.

Blessing:

May God, our Father, give you always your daily bread;
And may you share your bread daily with others.
May Jesus be the bread of your life;
And may you be the bread of Jesus for others.
May the Holy Spirit make you one with others,
As the many grains of that wheat are in one bread.
And may God bless you in the name of the Father,
And of the Son, and of the Holy Spirit.

Closing Song:

"Welcome Table"[7]
The children could be invited to wear their pilgrim hats as they proceed out of church.

References:

1. *The Fisherman's Surprise,* Alyce Bergey, Arch Books, Concordia Publishing House, 3558 Jefferson Avenue, St. Louis, Missouri 63118.

2. "Do You Really Love Me?" Carey Landry, *Hi, God* album; ASCAP; North American Liturgy Resources, 300 East McMillan Street, Cincinnati, Ohio 45219.

3. "We All Stand at Your Table," Joe Wise, *A New Day,* World Library of Sacred Music, 2145 Central Parkway, Cincinnati, Ohio 45214.

4. "Sons of God," Ray Repp, F.E.L. Publications, Inc., 1925 Pontius Avenue, Los Angeles, California 90025.

5. "Take Our Bread," Joe Wise, World Library of Sacred Music, 2145 Central Parkway, Cincinnati, Ohio 45214.

6. "Lord, By Your Cross," Joe Wise; *Welcome In;* ASCAP; North American Liturgy Resources, 300 East McMillan Street, Cincinnati, Ohio 45219.

7. "Welcome Table," Negro spiritual.

COMMUNITY LITURGY VI

Theme:

Community—Advent

Symbol:

Bakerwoman, Mary

Material Needed:

Enough clay or play dough for each child to make a small statue of Mary.

In keeping with the theme of this liturgy and after the experience of the Thanksgiving Liturgy, it would be good to make the statues with bread dough clay. Remove the crust from commercial bread and crumble the bread into a bowl. Add diluted Elmer's glue to form the right consistency. Keep the dough refrigerated when not being used. The statues can be painted after they have dried.

Preparation:

1) *Primary Preparation:*
Show the children episode #6 of the filmstrip series, *Kree Finds the Way.*[1] Discuss with the children the qualities that Kree remembered best in his mother. Encourage the children to relate these qualities to Mary.

Listen prayerfully with the children to the song, "The Bakerwoman."[2] Discuss the song with the children. You might want to have the bread-baking experience discussed in the Thanksgiving Liturgy in this book. Make bread clay as described above and invite each child to form a statue of Mary to be kept in a special place of honor in his own room.

2) *Other Suggestions:*
Special prayer services in honor of Mary. Make a special candle in honor of Mary, Mother of Light. Explain the significance of the candle and light it often and devoutly. Perhaps each child could be given a turn to light the candle for each class.

Encourage the children to get ready for the coming of Jesus by taking a special time each day to be quiet and listen to Jesus with Mary.

Read the book, *What Do Mothers Do?*[3] and then discuss with the children what Mary does for us. Form a rhythm band to play at this liturgy.

3) *Reflection:*
(for planner and children)
Mary, you are an advent in my life. You are always coming. You are never there. Because I do not understand you, I make no room for you in my inn. I'm sorry. Please come in and bake me the bread I need so badly.

THE LITURGY

Opening Song:

"The Bakerwoman" (verses 1 and 2, with rhythm band at chorus)
In the opening song, we ask Mary, in this liturgy, to bake for us the bread we need to be fed.

Greeting:

The celebrant welcomes the children, asking them to think of themselves as the bread that Mary is baking in this liturgy.

Penitential Rite:

For the times when we ignore Jesus. . .
For the times when we do not help other people to find Jesus. . .
For the times when we ignore other people. . .

Response:

Jesus, we are sorry.
For the Penitential Rite the children are seated comfortably and informally in a close group on the floor. The leader asks the children to close their eyes, bow their heads, and join hands with one another. The leader will read the Penitential Rite, asking the children to respond. (It would be better if the children, as a group, composed their own Penitential Rite and read it themselves.) Then the leader will invite the children to think of a time when they did not make Jesus present. If the children wish, they may express this aloud, with all the children responding.

Prayer:

God, you came to us once from Mary's body and love.
Help us to bring you to others in our bodies and in our love.
We love you forever and ever.

First Scripture Reading:

Isaiah 49:13, 15 (adapted)
Shout for joy, you heavens; exult, you earth!
You mountains, break into happy cries!
For God comforts his people, and feels sorry for those who are sad.

Does a woman forget her baby at the breast, or forget to love the child that came from her body?
Yet even if your mother could forget,
I will never forget you.

In the first scripture reading we reflect on the tremendous love that a mother has for her child.

Then we wonder at what great love Mary must have had for her Son who is love. We try to realize what great love Mary has for us who are one with her Son.

Additional Reading:

The Long Night (episode #6 of the series *Kree Finds the Way*)

Response:

(to the tune of "It's a Long Road to Freedom")[4]
It's a long night for children, waiting to be born; for you *are* our mother in the love of your Son, you carry us all and you bring us forth, the birth of light.

Gospel Acclamation:

"Alle, Alle"

Gospel:

Luke 1:5-2:18
See also: *Mary's Story*[5] (Luke 1:5-2:18 adapted)
In the Gospel we hear how Mary first began to bake the bread, Jesus.

Homily:

Suggestion:
Discuss with the children how Jesus is our bread. Talk about what Mary did for this bread. Help the children to think of ways in which they can bring this bread to people.

Prayer of the Faithful:

So that the poor people will find Jesus. . .
For the children whose mothers do not want them. . .
For the people who do not know Jesus in their hearts. . .

Response:

Father, hear our prayer.
(The children should be invited to add their own petitions.)

Offering:

The children will bring statues of Mary that they made from clay or dough. This is their sign of their love for Mary who brought Jesus to them and who loves them. After the liturgy the children will take these statues home and put them in a special place in their rooms to remind them of how wonderful Mary is and how much they want to be like her.

Offertory Song:

"The Bakerwoman" (verses 3 and 4; rhythm band at chorus)

Prayer Over the Gifts:

Lord, please take our statues of Mary, the bread, and the water and the wine. Make them into signs of your coming with us. We ask this in Jesus' name.

Preface:

Use Marian Preface.

Holy, Holy, Holy:

(sung)

Eucharistic Prayer:

(Choose the one the children relate to best.)

Acclamation:

(Sing "Lord, By Your Cross".)[6]

Amen:

(sung—The children might be invited to clap their hands in applause.)

Our Father:

(Join hands and recite.)

Rite of Peace:

An appropriate greeting would be: "Jesus be in you!"

Communion:

(under both species, if possible)

Communion Song:

"The Bakerwoman" (verses 5 and 6; rhythm band at chorus)

Thanksgiving:

Each one of us will think of a particular way in which Jesus has come into our lives. If we wish, we will thank him for this aloud.

Prayer:

Dear God, help us to be ready for you all the time that you come and help us too to be always ready to come with you to other people. We ask. . .

Blessing:

May you give birth to Jesus in your heart,
And may your heart be filled with love for others.

May you bear whatever sorrow you have,
With the patience of Mary.

May you always lift up your heart to God,
And may God lift up your head in joy.

And may God bless you in the name of the Father,
And of the Son, and of the Holy Spirit.

Closing Song:

"The Bakerwoman" (verse 6, sung twice; rhythm band at chorus)

Refreshments:

The rest of the communion bread not used in the liturgy, with honey butter, milk or punch. Coffee for adults.

References:

1. *Kree Finds the Way,* Sister M. Elizabeth, IHM, Sister M. Johnice, IHM, Roa's Films, Audio-Visuals for Catholic Education, Milwaukee, Wisconsin 53202.

2. "The Bakerwoman," *Go Tell Everyone,* Avant Garde Records, Inc., 250 W. 57th Street, New York, New York 10019.

3. *What Do Mothers Do?* Norma R. Knoche and Mary Voell Jones, Whitman Small World Library Book, Whitman Publishing Co., Racine, Wisconsin.

4. "It's a Long Road to Freedom," *Joy Is Like the Rain* album, Sister Miriam Therese Winter, Medical Mission Sisters, Avant Garde Records, Inc., 250 West 57th, New York, New York 10019.

5. *Mary's Story,* M. M. Brem, Arch Books, Concordia Publishing House, 3558 Jefferson Avenue, St. Louis, Missouri 63118.

6. "Lord, By Your Cross," Joe Wise *Welcome In;* ASCAP; North American Liturgy Resources, 300 East McMillan Street, Cincinnati, Ohio 45219.

COMMUNITY LITURGY VII

Theme:

Community—Christmas (culmination)

Symbol:

This is a summary of all the ideas used in the preceding liturgies of this section of the book. Symbols find fulfillment in the Incarnation. In this liturgy are: rock, tree, straw (in place of island), pumpkin seeds, bread, Mary.

Materials Needed:

Piece of brown paper (grocery bag) for each child

colored chalk

small pieces of construction paper to make packages

straw for crib

pumpkin seeds from jack-o'-lantern

bread (see Liturgy V of this section)

for a treat—cupcake for each child

small religious gift for each child

Preparation:

1) *Primary Preparation:*
Review the ideas of rock and friendship (Liturgy I).

Have the children streak their brown paper with the colored chalk. Crush the paper to form a rock. Fasten the rocks to a cardboard box to form the cave.

Review the ideas of tree and giving (Liturgy II).

Have the children cut little packages from construction paper to hang on the Giving Tree for each kind act that they do to prepare for the coming of Jesus.

Review the ideas of isolation and unity (Liturgy III).

Have the children make straw from construction paper or ask someone to bring real straw to be placed in the crib for each kind act performed to prepare for the coming of Jesus.

Review the ideas of jack-o'-lantern and hidden life within (Liturgy IV).

Have each child carefully take a seed that was saved from the jack-o'-lantern and place it in an envelope to be hidden under the rocks of the crib.

Review the ideas of bread and thanksgiving. Bake the bread for the Eucharist with the children (Liturgy V).

Review the ideas of Mary receiving the grain of wheat from God; kneading, baking, breaking, and giving the bread for us (Liturgy VI).

2) *Reflection:*
(for planner and children)
Mystery, and excitement, and love, that's what Christmas is. It is the greatest event in the life of a child. Children are Christmas people, full of mystery, excitement, and love. Christmas is the celebration of that for which we hoped, and planned, and dreamed, and waited, and worked, and struggled, and sacrificed, and prayed, and looked. From the beginning, man has longed for a God to be with him. We have been looking for the way to God with us in community. Now all our hope is fulfilled.

In our first liturgy, we celebrated God-with-us in our friendship and sharing with others. We saw the rock as a sign of friendship—strong, permanent, beautiful, unique, holdable, all-together. Making rocks for our crib reminded us that Jesus is with us in our friendship and sharing.

Our families are like trees—all giving life and support and wholeness to one another. Shel Silverstein's story of the Giving Tree showed us that Christ our Lord is the Giving Tree. The boy in the story took everything the tree had. At Christmas we give more to the tree than it ever had. We complete the tree as we complete the giving of Jesus. The tree, then, gives us light—Jesus.

Giving and love cannot grow unless it is reciprocal. We next celebrated our need for others. Completing that day's liturgy by singing for the people in the nursing home and bringing them our flower-favors, we understood that whatsoever we do for our brothers, that we do for Jesus. That day we used the island as a symbol of our need for others. Today we are using straw—straw, like an island, is just a piece afloat, unless it is attached deep in the ground, then it supports life.

Jesus came to give us the life that never dies. We buried our pumpkin seeds that look so dead under the rocks of the crib. They are a part of the crib, part of our Christmas, for we believe that our dead are still with us. We believe that when we plant the seeds in the spring, they will come to new life just as we will come to new life after death.

The bread that we have baked ourselves will become Jesus! Jesus will be born today on our altar just as truly as Mary gave birth to him in Bethlehem.

THE LITURGY

Opening Song:

"O Come, little Children"[1]
In the opening song of this liturgy, we call all God's children to come and witness the birth of Jesus today.

Greeting:

The celebrant welcomes the children who have worked so hard to make this Christmas celebration.

Penitential Rite:

For the times that we have not given to other people. . .
For the times we have not made other people happy. . .
For the times that we have disappointed you by not sharing with our brothers and sisters. . .

Response:

Jesus, we are sorry.
For the Penitential Rite the children are seated comfortably and informally in a close group on the floor. The leader asks the children to close their eyes, bow their heads, and join hands with one another. The leader will read the Penitential Rite, asking the children to respond. (It would be better if the children, as a group, composed their own Penitential Rite and read it themselves.) Then the leader will invite the children to think of a particular time when they did not make room for Jesus in their lives. If the children wish, they may express this aloud, with all the children responding.

Prayer:

God, you are the gift of love. Please help us to love you, to love the people you have made, and to love the whole world. We ask. . .

First Scripture Reading:

1 John 4:7-16
See also: *The Children's Living Bible*[4] paraphrased.
In this first scripture reading, we hear that God sent his only Son into the world for us because he loved us so much. When we love each other God lives in us and we live in God.

Response:

"Go Tell It on the Mountain"[2]

Gospel Acclamation:

"Alleluia! Praise the Lord!" (Chorus from "Thank You, Lord."[3])

Gospel:

The Baby Born in a Stable[4] (Luke 2:1-18)
In today's Gospel we hear the Good News—*Jesus is born*—this is what Christmas is all about.

Homily:

Suggestion:

Talk with the children about what Christmas means. Discuss how Jesus is being born today in themselves, in the world, in their homes, and in this liturgy.

Prayer of the Faithful:

For the people that will not have a happy Christmas. . .
For the people that do not know the real meaning of Christmas. . .
For our families and friends. . .

Response:

Lord, hear our prayer.
(The children should be invited to add their own petitions.)

Offering:

Each child will bring a straw for the crib or a small package for the tree, symbolic of the kind act he performed to get ready for the coming of Jesus.

Offertory Song:

"The Little Drummer Boy"[5]

Prayers Over the Gifts:

Lord, please take our acts of love with the bread and the water and the wine and transform them into yourself, for you are Jesus our brother.

Preface:

Christmas Preface

Holy, Holy, Holy:

(sung)

Eucharistic Prayer:

(Choose the one the children relate to best.)

Acclamation:

(sung—"Lord, By Your Cross")

107

Amen:

(sung—The children might be invited to clap their hands in applause.)

Our Father:

(Join hands and recite.)

Rite of Peace:

A good sign of peace would be the greeting: "Merry Christmas!"

Communion:

(under both species, if possible)

Communion Song:

"Silent Night"

Thanksgiving:

Our crib has no baby Jesus in it. Jesus is not being born in the crib. He is being born in us. Jesus is born in our hearts when we pray to him. We made our rocks to mean friendship and sharing and love for Jesus.

Sing:
(to the tune of "The Rock Holler,"[6] see Liturgy I, Part I.)
We bring our rocks; yes, Amen!
To show our love; yes, Amen!
Yes, Amen, Amen, Amen!

Read:
Jesus is born in the world when we do kind acts for people in the world. We put a straw in the crib for each kind act that we did.

Sing:
Whatsoever you do to the least of my brothers, that you do unto me.

Read:
When the crib was full we made little packages for our kind acts. Our kind acts made our Giving Tree into a Christmas tree.

Sing:
You can't be happy when you take, take, take;
You can't be happy when you hate, hate, hate;
You can be happy when you give what you make;
Hey! Give yourself away. ("She's Just an Old Stump," see Community Liturgy II.)

Read:
By giving to other people we are making Jesus be born.

Sing:

Bake us the bread; Mary, Mary.
Bake us the bread we need to be fed. ("The Bakerwoman," see Community Liturgy V.)

Prayer:

Dear God, thank you for giving us Jesus. We love you forever and ever.

Blessing:

May Jesus be your strong friend always;
And may you give to others as he gives to you.

May you eat with Jesus forever in the kingdom of heaven;
And may you fill others with his bread.

May you have a happy Christmas;
And may your Christmas never end.

And may God bless you in the name of the Father,
And of the Son, and of the Holy Spirit.

Closing Song:

"O Giving Tree" (to the tune of "O Christmas Tree")

Treats:

Cupcake ornamented with a small religious gift.

References:

1. "O Come Little Children," Joh. Abrah. Peter Schultz (1747-1800).

2. "Go Tell It On The Mountain," Negro spiritual.

3. "Thank You, Lord," Carey Landry, *Hi God* album, ASCAP; North American Liturgy Resources; 300 East McMillan Street, Cincinnati, Ohio 45219.

4. *The Baby Born in a Stable,* Janice Kramer, Arch Books, Concordia Publishing House, 3558 Jefferson Avenue, St. Louis, Missouri 63118.

5. "The Little Drummer Boy," unknown.

6. "The Rock Holler," *Run, Come, See* album, Robert Blue, FEL Publications, Ltd., 1925 Pontius Avenue, Los Angeles, California 90025.

COMMUNITY LITURGY VIII

Theme:

Community—Easter

Symbol:

Young Plant

Materials Needed:

pumpkin seeds from the jack-o'-lantern used in the Halloween liturgy
small milk carton or similar container for each child
sufficient potting soil for each container
two craft sticks for each child's cross
small craft rocks or similar objects for the children to paste on their
crosses to represent their love acts
empty egg shells and paints or other materials to decorate the Giving
Tree in an Easter theme

Preparation:

1) *Primary Preparation:*
Plant the pumpkin seeds at least two weeks before the liturgy. Make
this a devout, serious but joyful burial ceremony. Keep the containers
in a warm place and keep the soil moist. Once the plants are up they
will need light.

Show the children how to glue their craft sticks together in the form
of a cross.

Set up some system for gluing on the rocks or whatever you have
chosen to put on the cross to represent kind acts.

Decorate the Giving Tree.

Learn the words and gestures for the Prayer of the Faithful in this liturgy.

Learn a dance to do at the closing of this liturgy—*Lord of the Dance.*[1]

2) *Other Suggestions:*
You might take the children on a nature walk and help them to observe
all the signs of new life. If it is warm enough outdoors, you might let
the children lie down in the grass and absorb the smell of the new grass,
the warmth of the sun, and the feel of the fresh earth. Discuss the feel
of new life.

3) *Reflection:*
(for planner and children)
At Halloween we celebrated our individual identities. We saved the
seeds from our jack-o'-lantern. We carefully hid them under the rocks

110

of our Christmas crib to keep them with us. Two weeks before Easter we put the seeds in some soil in milk cartons, covered them with water, and put them in a warm place. Alleluia! The seeds that we once celebrated as our own identity are now alive with a new identity in Jesus— if we have really experienced conversion during Lent.

THE LITURGY

Opening Song:

"Alive, Alive"[2] (chorus only)
The children process in carrying their pumpkin plants. They set them on the altar. In the opening song of this liturgy we sing about how good it is to be alive, very much alive, and in love with life.

Greeting:

The celebrant welcomes the children and everyone claps hands in applause of life and in sheer joy of being alive.

Penitential Rite:

We grow when we see the wrong we have done, acknowledge our sinfulness, ask forgiveness, and forgive others.

For the Penitential Rite, the children are seated comfortably and informally in a close group on the floor. The leader will invite the children to think of something they have done for which they are sorry because it hindered the growth of the life of Jesus in them. The children will then express this aloud with all the children responding: Jesus, we are sorry.

Prayer:

Dear God, please help us always to grow in your love. Help us to grow by helping others to grow. In Jesus' name we pray.

First Scripture Reading:

Colossians 3:1-4 (adapted)
In the first scripture reading we see that our true life is hidden in Jesus just as the life of the pumpkin plant was hidden in the seed.

Since you have been brought to true life with Jesus, you must look for the true and the good things in life. Let your thoughts be on the things of God, for your true life is hidden with Jesus in God. But when Jesus is shown forth, and he is your real life—you will be shown forth too in all your glory with him. This is the Word of the Lord.

Additional Reading:

"Jay's Pumpkin"[3]
In the additional reading, Jay spends a great amount of time, effort, patience, and sacrifice on his pumpkin. We have to spend just as much on our spiritual life, if we want to grow.

Response:

(to the tune of "Run, Come See")[4]

Sing:

Run, come see the pumpkin growin',
Run, come see it growin' now;
Run, come see the pumpkin growin',
Run, come see and shout for joy.

Read:

A seed is a sign of Christ. Jesus said about himself: "Unless a grain of wheat falls on the ground and dies, it remains only a single grain; but if it dies it will become a great harvest" (John 12:24).

Sing:

Run, come see the Lord has risen . . .

Gospel Acclamation:

"Gospel Halleluia"[5]

Gospel:

Matthew 12:18-30
See also: *The Great Harvest*[6] (Matthew 12:18-30)

Homily:

Suggestion:
Helping the life of love to grow within us requires constant attention, work and sacrifice. Sometimes it seems that despite all our efforts, we produce nothing. But our good, like Jay's pumpkin, sometimes grows on the other side of the fence and is seen only by other people. Jesus told us to be good neighbors. Mr. Green was a good neighbor because he told Jay about his big pumpkin. We should tell other people about the good things we see them do. When we do this we make ourselves grow. By encouraging one another we can grow together by thirties, sixties, and even hundreds.

Prayer of the Faithful:

(Squat down, knees bent, arms surrounding knees.)
God our Father,
Help us to grow up straight and strong . . .
(Stand, raising arms straight up.)
Do not let us grow crooked . . .
(Arms stretched up, lean whole body to one side.)
Do not let us be blown by the winds of evil,
(Arms still extended, rotate whole body in circular motion.)
But help us to grow beautiful, inside and out,
(Lower arms in sweeping motion from bottom to top.)

Reaching up to you . . .
(Raise arms above.)
And out to our brothers . . .
(Extend arms sideways.)
Amen.

(Above prayer taken from a lecture by Jack Miffleton.)
Each child will bring a small wooden cross (craft sticks) he made and decorated with tiny rocks (craft rocks). The children placed a tiny rock on their crosses each time they made an act of friendship, a sacrifice, in thanksgiving for redemption.

Offertory Song:

"La, La, Life!"[7]

Prayer Over the Gifts:

Lord, accept our sacrifices and the water, the bread and the wine. Please make them help us to grow in your life.

Preface:

God, our Father, you are full of life, love, beauty, and goodness. We should praise you and thank you all the time because in Jesus, you bring all of us to fullness of life with you. And so with all the life there is in heaven and on earth we say:

Holy, Holy, Holy:

(sung)

Eucharistic Prayer:

(Choose the one the children relate to best.)

Acclamation:

(sung—"Lord, By Your Cross.")

Amen:

(sung—The children might be invited to clap their hands in applause.)

Our Father:

(Join hands and recite.)

Rite of Peace:

An appropriate greeting would be: Happy Easter! Peace be with you!

Communion:

(under both species, if possible)

Communion Song:

(to the tune of "Community Song")[8]
Communion means we are one; we are one; we are one. Communion means we are one; Alleluia!

Thanksgiving:

"Thank You Hymn"[9]

Blessing:

May you receive the grain of Jesus within you;
And may you work to let Jesus grow in you always.

May you enjoy a great harvest one day;
And may you share what you receive with others.

May you help others to grow;
And may you grow in the love of others.

And may God bless you in the name of the Father,
And of the Son, and of the Holy Spirit.

Commentary:

Life is sacred. Jesus said: "I came to make you more alive. To be alive is to feel and to touch, to laugh and to cry, to sing and to jump. Life is a dance with Jesus Christ before the face of God.

Closing Song:

"Lord of the Dance"[10]

Note:

Some of the pumpkin plants should be planted in a special plot where the children can help care for them. A pumpkin from these plants can be used in next year's Halloween liturgy, reinforcing the idea of continual growth. (My second-grade class plants the pumpkins in the spring. The harvest from the pumpkin plants is a gift to my new second-grade class the next fall. Our jack-o'-lantern then is always a very meaningful gift. We bake pumpkin pies and share them with others. We are now in the fourth generation of "Catholic" pumpkins.)

References:

1. *Lord of the Dance.*
2. "Alive, Alive," Album #2, *Life, Love, Joy,* Silver Burdett, General Learning Corporation, Morristown, New Jersey.
3. "Jay's Pumpkin," *More Friends and Neighbors,* Dorothy Baldwin, Scott, Foresman & Co., Chicago, Illinois.
4. *Run, Come See,* Robert Blue, F.E.L. Publications, Ltd., 1925 Pontius Avenue, Los Angeles, California 90025.

5. "Gospel Halleluia," *Run, Come See* album as above.
6. *The Great Harvest,* Gerald A. Pottebaum, Little People's Paperbacks, Geo. A. Pflaum, Publisher, Inc., Dayton, Ohio.
7. "La, La, Life!" *Come Out!* Miffleton and Blunt, World Library of Sacred Music, 2145 Central Parkway, Cincinnati, Ohio 45214.
8. "Community Song" *Run, Come See* album, Robert Blue, F.E.L. Publications, Ltd., 1925 Pontius Avenue, Los Angeles, California 90025.
9. "Thank You Hymn," *Run, Come See,* Robert Blue, F.E.L. Publications, Ltd., 1925 Pontius Avenue, Los Angeles, California 90025.
10. *Lord of the Dance.*

Additional Recommended Readings:

For Community Liturgy II

Readings:

A Tree Is Nice, Janice May Udry, Harper & Row, 10 E. 53rd Street, New York, New York 10022; record—Weston Woods Studios, Weston, Connecticut 06880.

The Easter Egg Tree, Katherine Milhous, Charles Scribner's Sons, 597 Fifth Avenue, New York, New York 10017.

A Tree For Peter, Kate Seredy, Viking Press, 625 Madison Avenue, New York, New York 10022.

Every Time I Climb a Tree, David McCord, *The Golden Treasury of Poetry,* Louis Untermeyer, Golden Press, New York.

Trees, Harry Behn, *The Arbuthnot Anthology of Children's Liturgy,* Arbuthnot, Scott, Foresman & Co., 1900 E. Lake Avenue, Glenview, Illinois 60025.

For Community Liturgy IIII

Readings:

Little Blue and Little Yellow, Leo Lionni, Astor-Honor, Inc., 67 Southfield Avenue, Stamford, Connecticut 06904.

Pepito's Story, Eugene Fern, Farrar, Straus & Giroux, Inc., 19 Union Square, W., New York, New York 10003.

Tico and the Golden Wings, Leo Lionni, Pantheon Books, Inc., 201 E. 50th Street, New York, New York 10022.

The Alphabet Tree, Leo Lionni, Pantheon Books, Inc., 201 E. 50th Street, New York, New York 10022.

Two Is a Team, Lorraine and Jerrold Beim, Harcourt, Brace & World, Inc., 757 Third Avenue, New York, New York 10017.

Snow Birthday, Helen Kay, Farrar, Straus & Giroux, Inc., 19 Union Square, W., New York, New York 10003.

The Wave, Margaret Hodges and Blair Lent, Houghton Mifflin Co., 2 Park Street, Boston, Massachusetts 02107.

Swimmy, Leo Lionni, Pantheon Books, Inc., 201 E. 50th Street, New York, New York 10022.

Crow Boy, Taro Yashima, Viking Press, Inc., 625 Madison Avenue, New York, New York 10022.

A Friend Is Someone Who Likes You, Joan Walsh Anglund, Harcourt, Brace & World, Inc., 757 Third Avenue, New York, New York 10017.

The Red Balloon, Albert Lamorisse, Doubleday & Co., Inc., 277 Park Avenue, New York, New York 10017.

The Night the Lights Went Out, unknown, Viking Press, 625 Madison Avenue, New York, New York 10022.

Recommended:

Kree Finds the Way[1] is a sound filmstrip series which presents in full-color contemporary art an introduction into the mysteries of faith through the experience of Christian living. Kree, the hero, is a simple boy with whom children from pre-school through grade six could easily identify. "His country is a strange faraway land which has no name on any map. It is a mysterious land and Kree is part of its mystery." This is a story of fast action, excitement and adventure. Rich in symbolism, it has many possible levels of depth. On one level, it is the story of the universal search of man for God. It is the story of any soul searching for God. Kree might be John of the Cross, Teresa of Avila, Augustine, Francis of Assisi, Teilhard de Chardin, or Thomas Merton. Kree is every child that is sincerely, albeit blindly and sinfully, responding to the call of God. Kree is beautiful because Kree is simple, humble, honest and sincere. Kree is human because Kree is proud; because he cries, sings, dances, fights, sins, loves. Kree is Christian because he is willing to change, willing to grow, willing to accept, willing to say, "I was wrong," or "I need you."

The set consists of 20 episodes. The series as a whole is of extremely high value in helping children to understand and appreciate not only the finding and celebrating of God in nature, but especially in Christian community and sacramental living. If these children's liturgies are used as a topical guide in a religious education program, it would be well to show Episodes #1-4 in conjunction with Chapter 4 of this book.

Episode #5 could be used as a summary of Chapter 4 and a lead into Chapter 5.

Episodes #6-12 should be shown as an introduction to the concept of community, fostering in the children a strong desire and sense of need for finding other people and sharing life with other people. Episode #6 will be used in the Advent Liturgy as a vivid expression of man's cry for man—for mother—for God.

Episodes #13-16 might be used in conjunction with the Easter Liturgy because in these episodes Kree experiences love, care, and growth in the context of a Christian community.

Episodes #14-17 could be used in conjunction with Chapters 5 and 6.

The culminating Episodes #18-20 could well provide a solid ground for understanding that the sign of the Eucharist—sharing in the body of Christ—can be truly celebrated fully only if the community understands and celebrates the sign of penance—forgiving and understanding one another and mutually nurturing growth in Christ.

References:

1. *Kree Finds the Way,* Sister M. Elizabeth, I.H.M., Sister M. Johnice, I.H.M., Roa's Films, Audio-Visuals for Catholic Education, Milwaukee, Wisconsin 53202.

Chapter 6

FOUR MODEL CHILDREN'S LITURGIES
FOR GRADES 4, 5 and 6

Introduction

The following four liturgies are for grades four, five and six. The preparation involved in these models is a different type from that suggested in the previous two chapters. These require a little more reflection and less activity.

When children get older, they need fewer "things" to help them celebrate. Even at the relatively young age of nine, 10, or 11 years they can understand the poetry of Rod McKuen, or the message of the song "Ebb Tide."

As with the previous sections, these are only model liturgies, and they reflect where a specific community of people were at a specific time. They are not to be used again, but rather are the source of ideas for another community.

UPPER GRADES LITURGY I

Theme:

Water: the power of life and death

Symbol:

Water

Opening Song:

"Joy Is Like the Rain"[1]

Introduction:

Water is necessary for life, yet it can destroy the very life it nourishes. Let us celebrate water in our lives.

Penitential Rite:

For seeing water only as a means to get somewhere . . .
For allowing the graces of Baptism to go unused . . .
For not turning to God when we were thirsty for life . . .
For the times we were not a bridge over someone else's troubled
    waters . . .

Response:

Lord, wash me with your love.

Prayer:

Jesus, you were a sailor. You know water meant real life. Help us to
be forgiven and drenched in your love.

First Reading:

Suggestion 1—"And you want to travel with him" by Leonard Cohen[2]
Suggestion 2—John 7:37-38
During the reading play the record, *Bridge Over Troubled Waters*,[3] as a
soft background.

Response:

Silence, just sit and listen to ourselves for a while.

Gospel Acclamation:

Sing "Come to Springs of Living Water."[4]

Gospel:

John 4:13-14 (Christ is the living water.)

Homily:

Show how our Baptism comes alive only when we make it.

Prayer of the Faithful:

For all baptized people . . .
For those whose lives are threatened or taken
by floods, storms, drowning . . .
For our parents, who shared their faith with us,
in our Baptism . . .

Response:

Lord, bring your life to us.

Offering:

To show our willingness to become alive in Christ's Spirit, we will approach the water and sign each other on the forehead with the sign of

the cross saying, "I sign you with the (life, peace) of Christ."

Offertory Song:

"The Spirit Is a 'Movin' "[5]

Prayer Over the Gifts:

Thank you Lord for your gifts of water and the Spirit. It helps us to know why we offer these gifts of bread and wine to you, through Jesus your Son. Amen.

Preface:

Of the Spirit or #4

Holy, Holy, Holy:

(sung)

Eucharistic Prayer:

#2 or #4

Eucharistic Acclamation:

#1 (sung)

Amen:

(sung)

Our Father:

(Join hands and recite.)

Rite of Peace:

Welcome each other into a new life with Christ.

Lamb of God:

(recited)

Communion:

(under both forms)

Communion Song:

"Spirit of God"

Thanksgiving:

Sing "Without Clouds"[6] (from *Walk to That Gloryland* by the Damiens), or read it as a poem with water music softly playing in the background.

Prayer:

Father, now we know that water brings us life and you are the life it brings through Christ, your Son and our brother, Amen.

Blessing:

(Use holy water in final blessing.)

Closing Song:

"This Land Is Your land"[7]
Alternative: "Joy, Joy, Joy"[8]

References:

Liturgy I

1. "Joy Is Like the Rain," Medical Mission Sisters, Vanguard Music Corp., 250 W. 57th Street, New York, New York 10019.

2. *Listen to Love,* ed. Louis M. Savary, S.J., Regina Press, New York, 1968 (p. 114).

3. *Bridge Over Troubled Waters,* Paul Simon, Charing Cross Music Inc., 114 E. 55th Street, New York, New York 10022.

4. "Come to Springs of Living Water," Medical Mission Sisters, Vanguard Music Corp., 250 W. 57th Street, New York, New York 10019.

5. "The Spirit Is a 'Movin'," Carey Landry, North American Liturgy Resources, 300 E. McMillan Avenue, Cincinnati, Ohio 45219.

6. "Without Clouds," Darryl Ducote, F.E.L. Publications Ltd., 1925 Pontius Avenue, Los Angeles, Calif. 90025.

7. "This Land Is Your Land," Ludlow Music Inc., Suite 2160, 10 Columbus Circle, New York, New York 10019.

8. "Joy, Joy, Joy," traditional gospel song; Additional verses by Carey Landry, North American Liturgy Resources, 300 E. McMillan Avenue, Cincinnati, Ohio 45219.

UPPER GRADES LITURGY II

Theme:

God speaks to me in rivers, lakes and sea.

Preparation:

Listen to the song "Ebb Tide."[1] Have a net and hourglass, shells, etc. Everyone writes down what he hears and sees in these symbols of the sea. Share a few of these ideas with everyone, responding after each, "It is the Lord."

Opening Song:

"It's a Long Road to Freedom"[2]

Introduction:

The celebrant greets the children with the calmness of the sea. We can draw closer to God by understanding his creation. During this liturgy, walk along with Jesus and see if you can recognize him in the breaking of the bread.

Penitential Rite:

For the times we have not recognized Christ in nature . . .
For fearing the storms in the sea of life . . .
For not casting our nets out to others . . .

Response:

Jesus, forgive us.

Prayer:

Lord, we want to be able to say, "It is the Lord." Help us to know you in whatever way you appear to us. This we ask through Jesus, who appears to us as the Son of God. Amen.

First Reading:

Read "Fish Story," p. 57 in *Stillpoint*.[3]

Response:

Have several people give (spontaneous or prepared) responses to these: The sea gives me . . .

I give back to the sea . . .

Gospel Acclamation:

Alleluia—Come and I will make you fishers of men . . .
Alleluia—(alleluias sung—verse recited)

Gospel:

Christ appears to his apostles by the sea (John 21:4-14).

Prayer of the Faithful:

Thank you for giving us the sea to wash away our hurts . . .
For those who haven't cast out their nets for God . . .

Response:

Reach us, Lord
Lord, hear our prayer

Offering:

Offer a symbol of the sea (shell, net, etc.).

Offertory Song:

"Take Care to Wonder"[4]

Prayer Over the Gifts:

Lord, take the sea, this bread and wine, but most of all Lord, take us.
Make us a real part of your life.

Preface:

Of the season

Holy, Holy, Holy:

(sung)

Eucharistic Prayer:

#2

Eucharistic Acclamation:

#1 (sung)

Amen:

(sung)

Our Father:

(recited)

Rite of Peace:

Exchange some symbols of rivers, lakes or the sea.

Lamb of God:

(recited)

Communion:

(under both forms)

Communion Song:

"Spirit of God"[5]

Thanksgiving:

Play sea music and read a poem about the sea.

Prayer:

Lord, you helped your apostles to recognize you. Help us see you in your body and blood. Continue to appear to us through nature.

Blessing:

Special blessing from Sacramentary for 3rd Sunday after Easter

Closing Song:

"Joy Is Like the Rain"[6]

References:

Liturgy II

1. "Ebb Tide," Robbins Music Corp., New York, New York.

2. "It's A Long Road to Freedom," Medical Mission Sisters, Vanguard Music Corp., 250 W. 57th Street, New York, New York 10019.

3. *Stillpoint—He Is the Stillpoint of the Turning Word,* Mark Link, S.J., Argus Communications, Chicago, Illinois 60657.

4. "Take Care to Wonder," (Wonderful World) James Thiem, F.E.L. Publications, Ltd., 1925 Pontius Avenue, Los Angeles, California 90025.

5. "Spirit of God," Medical Mission Sisters, Vanguard Music Corp., 250 W. 57th Street, New York, New York 10019.

6. "Joy Is Like the Rain," Medical Mission Sisters, Vanguard Music Corp., 250 W. 57th Street, New York, New York 10019.

UPPER GRADES LITURGY III

Theme:

Do something beautiful for God; set theme by reading "Do Something Beautiful for God" by James Turro:

Preparation:

Reflect on "Do Something Beautiful for God"[1]
Let someone
feel the rich warmth
of your love.
You will be revealing
something of God
thereby.
God,
to be sure,
is love
and you must not be content
merely to say so
but in your actions
you must bear
that same witness.
Actions
speak louder
than words
—this is as true
when you are trying
to bring God home
to people
as at any other time.

REFLECTIONS . . . . James Turro

Opening Song:

"They'll Know We Are Christians"[2]
Alternative—"Come My Brothers"[3]

Introduction:

Do everything in the spirit of celebrating God's love which is shown by the way we love one another.

Penitential Rite:

Because there have been times when we haven't loved one another, let's turn to one another now and say we are sorry.

Prayer:

Father, you know our need for forgiveness. May we learn how to say "I'm sorry" and mean it.

First Reading:

The measure of your love for Christ is the love you have for the person you love least.

Suggestion 1—Read the poem "An Outstretched Hand"[4] by Rod McKuen.

> Each of us was made by God
> and some of us grew tall.
> Others stood in the wind
> their branches bent and fell.
> Those of us who walk in light
> must help the ones in darkness up.
> For that's what life is all about
> and love is all there is to life.
>
> Each of us was made by God
> beautiful in his mind's eye.
> Those of us that turned out sound
> should look across our shoulders once
> and help the weak ones to their feet.
>
> It only takes an outstretched hand.

Have the children place the hand they made as a name tag on another person saying, "I give my hand to you in friendship."

or

Suggestion 2: Matthew 5:44-46 (loving one another)
Matthew 18:21-22 (how often to forgive someone)

Response:

Sing or recite:
I'm in love with my God.
My God's in love with me.
The more I love you,
the more I know
I'm in love with my God.[5]

Gospel:

Christ's command—love one another: John 15:10-17 or Matthew 22:35-39

Homily:

Some of the ways we can make Christ's love known

Prayer of the Faithful:

For the person I love the least. . .
That we may do something beautiful for God. . .

For people who don't know the love of Christ. . .
Other needs. . .

Response:

Lord, help us to love.

Offering:

Each person places his hand on the altar as a sign that he is willing to do something beautiful for God.

Offertory Song:

"Follow Christ"[6]
Alternative: "Of My Hands"[7] or "Take My Hands"[8]

Prayer Over the Gifts:

Lord, receive with outstretched hands our gifts of bread and wine. Teach us to love you and others through this offering.

Preface:

Simplest one possible.

Holy, Holy, Holy:

(sung)

Eucharistic Prayer:

#2

Eucharistic Acclamation:

(sung)

Amen:

(sung)

Our Father:

If we love our brother, we should be able to join hands and pray with confidence to the Father the words Christ taught us. . .

Rite of Peace:

Say, "May you know God's love" or "God's love be with you."

Lamb of God:

(sung, if possible)

Communion:

(under both forms)

Communion Song:

"Whatsoever You Do"[9]
Alternative: "Try a Little Kindness"[10]

Thanksgiving:

Each thanks God for someone he loves.

Prayer:

Christ, you have revealed to us how much God is love. We want to go now and love everyone, so that the world will know God, who is love.

Closing Song:

"Pass It On"[11] or "Less of Me"[12]

Project:

Have children trace their hands on a piece of paper and write on it: "I give you my hand" and their names. Give them a pin or a piece of masking tape, so they can make a name tag during Mass.

References:

Liturgy III

1. "Do Something Beautiful for God," James Turro, from *Reflections . . . Path to Prayer,* Paulist Press, Paramus, New Jersey 07652. With Permission.

2. "They'll Know We Are Christians," Peter Scholtes, F.E.L. Publications, Ltd., 1925 Pontius Avenue, Los Angeles, California 90025.

3. "Come My Brothers," Ray Repp; F.E.L. Publications, 1925 Pontius Avenue, Los Angeles, California 90025.

4. "An Outstretched Hand," Rod McKuen, from *Lonesome Cities,* Random House, New York, New York. With permission.

5. "I'm in Love with My God," ("Malieta's Song") Joe Wise, World Library Publications, Inc., 2145 Central Parkway, Cincinnati, Ohio 45214. With permission.

6. "Follow Christ," Sebastian Temple, St. Francis Productions, 1229 Santee Street, Los Angeles, California 90015.

7. "Of My Hands," Ray Repp, F.E.L. Publications, Ltd., 1925 Pontius Avenue, Los Angeles, Calif. 90025.

8. "Take My Hands," Sebastian Temple, St. Francis Productions, 1229 Santee Street, Los Angeles, California 90015.

9. "Whatsoever You Do," Rev. W. F. Jabusch, ACTA Foundation, 4848 N. Clark Street, Chicago, Illinois 60640.

10. "Try A Little Kindness," Glen Campbell Music, Inc., 10920 Wilshire Boulevard, Los Angeles, California 90024.

11. "Pass It On," Kurt Kaiser, Lexicon Music, Inc., Woodland Hills, California.

12. "Less of Me," Glen Campbell Music, Inc., 10920 Wilshire Boulevard, Los Angeles, California 90024.

UPPER GRADES LITURGY IV

Theme:

Look beyond our walls (hardness, prejudice), Lord, and help us see.

Preparation:

Pass out rocks (or anything from nature). Read the poem "To Look at Any Thing" by John Moffitt.[1]

> To look at any thing,
> If you would know that thing,
> You must look at it long:
> To look at this green and say
> "I have seen spring in these
> Woods" will not do—you must
> Be the thing you see:
> You must be the dark snakes of
> Stems and ferny plumes of leaves,
> You must enter in
> To the small silences between
> The leaves,
> You must take your time
> And touch the very peace
> They issue from.
> John Moffitt

Then have them think about that object of nature. Read this poem written by a fifth-grader.

> I am a rock
> full of love.
> I want to
> make friends.
> People fall
> over me.
> Some pick me up
> and put me in their pockets.
> Others
>   drop me.

Reflect on any of these scripture readings:

1. Parable of the barren fig tree (cutting down people who seem unable to do anything or who are "dumb")—Luke 13:6-9

2. Christ's understanding of the woman caught in adultery—John 7:53-8:11

131

Have them tell what their rock says to them of destruction, e.g., passing judgment, condemning, forgetting or neglecting others, gossiping, nagging, accusing unjustly. Then have them contrast those thoughts with a rock as a symbol of support, security, fidelity.

Listen to "Christ Is My Rock."[2]

Opening Song:

"I Am a Rock"[3]
Alternative: "Lord, Teach Us to Pray"[4]

Introduction:

Sometimes we allow ourselves to put up walls because we don't like someone or we are afraid of something.

But to look at that person long enough to see the beauty is the task we *celebrate* today.

Penitential Rite:

For seeing the splinter in another's eye, and not seeing the plank in my own eye. . .
For judging what's on the outside of people. . .
For going inside myself and putting up a wall, so no one can see who I am. . .
For going through a whole day without looking at the beauty in someone or something. . .

Response:

Lord, that I may see.
Alternative: Lord, help us look beyond.

Prayer:

Lord, we want the peace and love that come to us through beauty—the quiet joy in someone's smiling eyes, in a sleeping child, in a leaf blown across our feet. Help us to look beyond what life and people seem to be. We ask this through Christ, who always saw the good in others. Amen.

Gospel Acclamation:

Sing "Allelu" (Ray Repp).[5]

Gospel:

A good man draws what is good from the store of goodness in the heart—Luke 6:39-45.

Homily:

(celebrant's choice)

Prayer of the Faithful:

Thank you for creating things for us to see. . .

For all those people we've hurt by throwing rocks at them. . .

For anyone who feels alone and hard, like a rock. . .

For all those people who have helped us look beyond and see goodness. . .

Other needs. . .

Response:

Look beyond our hardness, Lord, and help us see.

Gifts:

Bring up rocks.

Offering:

Have each person offer his rock. (They could sing "Of My Rock I
Give to You" . . . to the tune of "Of My Hands.")

Alternative: Walk up to the altar and tell God that "Today I am going
to see the good in . . . my brother, the sky, etc."

Offertory Song:

"Of My Hands"[6]

Prayer Over the Gifts:

Lord, take our gifts. We want to give back to you all the goodness you
have created. Help us to see more through this Mass.

Preface:

Eucharistic Prayer #4

Holy, Holy, Holy:

(sung)

Eucharistic Prayer:

#3

Eucharistic Acclamation:

#3 (sung)

Amen:

(sung)

Our Father:

(sung)

Rite of Peace:

Each person can offer a rock to another as a sign of his desire to be living, supportive stones to one another, saying, "May the strength of God's peace be yours" or "May you find peace in looking at others."

Lamb of God:

(sung)

Communion:

(under both forms)

Communion Song:

"Look Beyond"[7]
Alternative: "Today"[8] or "Prayer of St. Francis"[9]

Thanksgiving:

Let's take some moments to look with the quiet eyes of our minds, thinking of the beauty in others and thank God for his goodness that makes us happy.

Prayer:

Christ, you never condemned anyone. You could look through everything and see goodness there. Thank you for your body and blood. It helps us be strong. Stay with us always.

Closing Song:

"In the Stars"[10]
Alternative: "God Gives His People Strength"[11]

Project:

Paint rocks.

References:

Liturgy IV

1. © 1961 by John Moffitt. Reprinted from his volume, *The Living Seed,* by permission of Harcourt Brace Jovanovich, Inc.

2. "Christ Is My Rock," Medical Mission Sisters, Vanguard Music Corp., 250 W. 57th Street, New York, New York 10019.

3. "I Am a Rock," Charing Cross Music, Inc., 114 E. 55th Street, New York, New York 10022.

4. "Lord, Teach Us to Pray," Joe Wise, World Library Publications, Inc. 2145 Central Parkway, Cincinnati, Ohio 45214.

5. "Allelu," Ray Repp, F.E.L. Publications, Ltd., 1925 Pontius Avenue, Los Angeles, California 90025.

6. "Of My Hands," Ray Repp, F.E.L. Publications, Ltd., 1925 Pontius Avenue, Los Angeles, California 90025.

7. "Look Beyond," Darryl Ducote, F.E.L. Publications, Ltd., 1925 Pontius Avenue, Los Angeles, California 90025.

8. "Today," Randy Sparks, Miller Music Corp., 1540 Broadway, New York, New York 10036.

9. "Prayer of St. Francis," Sebastian Temple, St. Francis Publications, 1229 Santee Street, Los Angeles, California 90015.

10. "In the Stars," (*He's Everything to Me*), Ralph Carmichael, Lexicon Music, Inc., Woodland Hills, California.

11. "God Give His People Strength," Sister Winter, Medical Mission Sisters, Vanguard Music Corp., 250 W. 57th Street, New York, New York 10019.

APPENDIX

Explanation and Commentary on Directory for Masses with Children

In 1969, the Congregation for Divine Worship published the General Instruction of the *Revised Roman Missal.* At that time the congregation began work on a supplement to that instruction for "Masses with Children," which was published November 1, 1973. It is this supplement which is the subject of these pages. As with all Roman directories, this one is general in tone, and eventually specific adaptations must be made by the national conferences of bishops in each country. The age group concerned in this directory is below pre-adolescence (i.e., below junior high), although many of its suggestions are applicable in junior high or even above.

The document is roughly divided into three major sections: 1) Introduction and explanation; 2) Masses with adults at which children also participate, 3) Masses with children and only a few adults.

Introduction and Explanation

The directory begins by discussing the theological and pastoral concepts of children's liturgies and gives an explanation of what they are.

The Mass, the celebration of the Paschal Mystery, is to be shared by all the faithful. We believe in Baptism, and so we believe that the graces of Baptism are present in people of all ages. We can all be in communion with Christ, and we can all celebrate him in the liturgy.

In addition to the theological need and right of all the baptized to share the liturgy in a way they can understand, the directory goes further to say that liturgical formation of children must be linked together with general human growth and development as well as Christian education. In other words, liturgy is not just for adults, nor are adult liturgies adequate for children.

137

During the last few years in this country and elsewhere, great debate has taken place on whether or not children should have adapted rites for Mass, or, to put it another way, whether or not children's liturgies should be an essential part of the lives of children. The document seems to state clearly the supreme importance of good children's liturgies, putting great pressure on those priests and parishes who have so far refused to adapt the Mass. But on the other hand, it speaks of adaptation rather than new rites, responding to those who contend the Mass is only a prayer for adults, and who have advocated completely new prayer forms for children.

Two major emphases stand out in the introduction: the need for children's liturgies to be an integral part of religious education programs—and the need for parental and home involvement in the growing liturgical and ritual awareness of children.

In both of these areas the new religious education texts and programs, especially the Green Bay Plan and the Idaho Plan, are already doing great work. Many more helps and aids can be expected in the near future, both from religious education sources and from family life sources. Before this document can have a major effect on American life, much more extensive adult and family religious education may be presented.

The introduction concludes with a strong encouragement of para-liturgical services, such as bible services, penance services and devotional rites which ultimately promote better liturgy.

Masses with Adults in
Which Children Also Participate

While this section is not the main point of the directory, it is the goal toward which children's liturgies are directed—full involvement of the entire Christian community.

Basically three things are said: 1) Praying, participating adults have a great effect on children and vice versa. 2) Families should attend together if possible, with infants brought in for the final blessing if they are being taken care of elsewhere. 3) The ministers of the liturgy should definitely acknowledge and take into account the presence of children, even to the extent of dividing the congregation for the Liturgy of the Word, if necessary.

Masses with Children in Which
Only a Few Adults Participate

The major thrust of the document is in Chapter 3 where detailed permissions and regulations are explained. First of all the document states clearly that special Masses with children are necessary, and adaptation is essential. These Masses are not the totality of the liturgical life of children, but rather are to promote and strengthen the ability of children to participate in Sunday parish liturgy. Obviously this requires that the Sunday liturgy contains areas to which the children can relate, and this is the responsibility of the parish priests and parish liturgy committee. This chapter is divided into a number of sections.

1. *Offices and Ministries in the Celebration*

This very important section can be best understood by quoting paragraph No. 22:

"The principles of active and conscious participation are in a sense even more valid for Masses celebrated with children. Every effort should be made to increase the participation and to make it more intense. For this reason as many children as possible should have special parts in the celebration, for example: preparing the place and the altar, acting as cantor, singing in a choir, playing musical instruments, proclaiming the readings, responding during the homily, reciting the intentions of the general intercessions, bringing the gifts to the altar, and performing similar activities in accord with the usage of various communities.

"To encourage participation it will sometimes be helpful to have several additions, for example, the insertion of motives for giving thanks before the priest begins the dialogue of the Preface."

As can be seen from this quotation, Rome makes it very clear that children are to be given their right to participate. This is coupled with a strong insistence on the preparation of the priest, and hard work on his part to understand the uniqueness of children's liturgies. "It is the responsibility of the priest who celebrates with children to make the celebration festive, fraternal and meditative" (No. 23). The priest is encouraged to use his own words for some parts of the Mass, to accomplish better the goal of true worship. Much more is demanded of priests by this document than was demanded in the past.

Encouraged also is the active participation of those adults who are present, and as more than just monitors. They should take an active role, even to the extent of speaking after the Gospel, if the pastor so requests.

2. Place and Time of Celebration

The time and place of liturgy are important. Liturgy should be celebrated at the time of the day when the children are most open to God; and not every day with the same group lest they weary, or not have adequate time to plan or prepare.

The primary place for children's liturgies is within the church building but the goal is always the same, to celebrate in "a place where the children can conduct themselves freely according to the demands of a living liturgy that is suited to their age" (No. 25).

The group which celebrates should not be too large, lest the possibilities of participation be lessened. Again paraliturgies are encouraged.

3. *Preparation for the Liturgy and Singing*

Another of the most important paragraphs in the directory is No. 29:

"Each Eucharistic celebration with children should be carefully prepared beforehand, especially with regard to prayers, songs, readings and intentions of the general intercessions. This should be done in discussion with the adults and with the children who will have a special ministry in these Masses. If possible, some of the children should take part in preparing and ornamenting the place of celebration and preparing the chalice with the paten and the cruets. Over and above the appropriate internal participation such activity will help to develop the spirit of community celebration."

Part of this essential preparation is music. Singing is to be encouraged, especially the singing of the acclamations. The texts of some parts of the liturgy may be adapted if musical requirements demand.

Greatest emphasis should be placed on the children playing instruments, but the use of "technically produced" music (i.e., records and tapes) is permitted. Care should be taken that the music enhances the liturgy, rather than detracts.

4. *Gestures, Actions, Visual Elements, and Silence*

The liturgy is to be an activity of the whole self, and the actions and gestures of the Mass should promote this. The document requests that the bishops study the various gestures of their respective cultures with an eye to specific adaptations.

Priests are expected to take special notice and care of their gestures in order that the meaning is truly conveyed. Special gestures and actions by children are encouraged, especially the use of various types of processions.

Active participation is enhanced by the creative use of many different types of visual elements, both traditional ones such as candles, vestments, the cross, etc., and other types of visual elements, such as banners, lights, and drawings.

One of the more essential elements of any good liturgy, including children's liturgy, is the effective use of silence. There should be an introduction to and explanation of the reason for silence, and what should be done with it.

5. *The Parts of the Mass*

Each part of the Mass is unique; in children's liturgy there should be a recognition and appreciation of that. Some few parts, i.e., acclamations, the Lord's Prayer, the Sign of the Cross, and responses should not be adapted, lest there be too little similarity between Sunday and children's liturgies. Adaptations are permitted in the rest of the Mass.

Introductory Rites

The simplicity and purposes of the introductory rites are well expressed. "The introductory rite of Mass has the purpose 'that the faithful, assembling in unity, should constitute a communion and should prepare themselves properly for hearing the Word of God and celebrating the Eucharist worthily" (General Instruction, No. 24). Therefore every effort should be made to create this disposition in the children and to avoid any excess of rites in this part of the Mass.

"It is sometimes proper to omit one or the other element of the introductory rite or perhaps to enlarge one of the elements. There should always be at least some introductory element, which is completed by the opening prayer or collect. In choosing individual elements one should be careful that each one be used at times and that none be entirely neglected" (No. 40).

This new permission to drop sections of the introductory rites is an important advance over previous legislation.

The Word of God

As in most Roman documents on liturgy, the section on biblical readings is somewhat complicated. What it says can be reduced to a number of points: 1) There always is to be bible reading. 2) The reading should fit the children, and may be from any part of the bible. 3) The planners should try to have two readings (on Sunday three readings), but if children cannot understand the assigned reading, you may have just one, but it must be from the Gospel. 4) Use translations of scripture rather than paraphrases. 5) Psalmody, and/or alleluias should be sung between readings (or after the homily if there is only one reading). 6) Commentaries and introductions are essential. 7) Dividing the readings into parts for choral reading is encouraged (as in the Holy Week Passion reading). 8) The bishops should prepare a lectionary for children.

Some of these permissions are new, and are greatly needed.

The homily should be well prepared, and dialogue homilies are encouraged. The Apostles' Creed may be used rather than the Nicene Creed.

Presidential Prayers

The priest is now permitted to choose from the Roman Missal any of the prayers, and may even adapt them. They should not violate the literary genre of presidential prayers lest they become moral exhortation or childish speech.

The Eucharistic Prayer is a center of worship and should be prayed clearly. The active singing of the children in the acclamations (Holy, Amen) is essential. As for the texts of the Eucharistic Prayer itself, the document is clear: "For the present, the four Eucharistic Prayers approved by the supreme authority for Masses with adults are to be employed and kept in liturgical use until the Apostolic See makes other provisions for Masses with children" (No. 52).

Communion and the Following Rites

After the Eucharistic Prayer, the Lord's Prayer, the Breaking of Bread, and the Invitation to Communion should always follow. The children should be prepared for Communion and the rites should emphasize the significance of the reception of Jesus Christ. When possible there should be singing during the Communion procession.

Before the final blessing, there should be a summary of the liturgy, with repetition and application of what the children have heard.

Conclusion

The document is a major effort to promote and encourage the liturgical participation of children. It supports the type of children's liturgies presently being celebrated throughout the country. For the most part, the restrictions are valid and easily understood to be necessary. The new permissions, such as one reading, or omitting some introductory rites, are certainly most welcome. No good parish priest can afford to ignore the implications of the document.

The final paragraph of the directory expresses well the intention of Rome: "The contents of the directory are intended to help children quickly and joyfully to encounter Christ together in the eucharistic celebration and to stand in the presence of the Father with him. If they are formed by conscious and active participation in the eucharistic sacrifice and meal, they should learn day by day, at home and away from home, to proclaim Christ to others among their family and among their peers, by living the 'faith, which expresses itself through love' (Galatians 5-6)" (No. 55).

DIRECTORY FOR MASSES WITH CHILDREN

INTRODUCTION

1.   The Church shows special concern for baptized children who have yet to be fully initiated through the sacraments of confirmation and eucharist as well as for children who have only recently been admitted to holy communion. Today the circumstances in which children grow up are not favorable to their spiritual progress.[1] In addition, sometimes parents barely fulfill the obligations of Christian education which they undertake at the baptism of their children.

2.   In bringing up children in the Church a special difficulty arises from the fact that liturgical celebrations, especially the eucharist, cannot fully exercise their innate pedagogical force upon children.[2] Although the mother tongue may now be used at Mass, still the words and signs have not been sufficiently adapted to the capacity of children.

In fact, even in daily life children cannot always understand everything that they experience with adults, and they easily become weary. It cannot be expected, moreover, that everything in the liturgy will always be intelligible to them. Nonetheless, we may fear spiritual harm if over the years children repeatedly experience in the Church things that are scarcely comprehensible to them: recent psychological study has established how profoundly children are formed by the religious experience of infancy and early childhood, according to their individual religious capacity.[3]

3.   The Church follows its Master, who "put his arms around the children . . . and blessed them" (Mark 10:16). It cannot leave children to themselves. The Second Vatican Council had spoken in the Constitution on the Liturgy about the need of liturgical adaptation for various groups.[4] Soon afterwards, especially in the first Synod of Bishops held in Rome in 1967, the Church began to consider how participation of children could be made

143

easier. On the occasion of the Synod the president of the Consilium for the Implementation of the Constitution on the Liturgy said explicitly that it could not be a matter of "creating some entirely special rite but rather of retaining, shortening, or omitting some elements or of making a better selection of texts."[5]

4.   All the details of eucharistic celebration with a congregation were determined in the General Instruction of the revised *Roman Missal,* published in 1969. Then this congregation began to prepare a special directory for Masses with children, as a supplement to the instruction. This was done in response to repeated petitions from the entire Catholic world and with the cooperation of men and women specialists from almost every nation.

5.   Like the General Instruction, this directory reserves some adaptations to conferences of bishops or individual bishops.[6]

With regard to adaptations of the Mass which may be necessary for children in a given country but which cannot be included in this general directory, the conferences of bishops should submit proposals to the Apostolic See, in accord with article 40 of the Constitution on the Liturgy. These adaptations are to be introduced only with the consent of the Apostolic See.

6.   The directory is concerned with children who have not yet entered the period of pre-adolescence. It does not speak directly of children who are physically or mentally retarded because a broader adaptation is sometimes necessary for them.[7] Nevertheless, the following norms may also be applied to the retarded, with the necessary changes.

7.   The first chapter of the directory (nos. 8-15) gives a kind of foundation by considering the different ways in which children are introduced to the eucharistic liturgy. The second chapter briefly treats Masses with adults, in which children also take part (nos. 16-19). Finally, the third chapter (nos. 20-54) treats at greater length Masses with children, in which only some adults take part.

CHAPTER I

The Introduction of Children to the Eucharistic Celebration

8.   A fully Christian life cannot be conceived without participation in the liturgical services in which the faithful, gathered into a single assembly, celebrate the paschal mystery. Therefore, the religious initiation of children must be in harmony with this purpose.[8] By baptizing infants, the Church expresses its confidence in the gifts received from this sacrament; thus it must be concerned that the baptized grow in communion with Christ and the brethren. Sharing in the eucharist is the sign and pledge of this very

communion. Children are prepared for eucharistic communion and introduced more deeply into its meaning. It is not right to separate such liturgical and eucharistic formation from the general human and Christian education of children. Indeed it would be harmful if liturgical formation lacked such a foundation.

9.   For this reason all who have a part in the formation of children should consult and work together. In this way even if children already have some feeling for God and the things of God, they may also experience the human values which are found in the eucharistic celebration, depending upon their age and personal progress. These values are the activity of the community, exchange of greetings, capacity to listen and to seek and grant pardon, expression of gratitude, experience of symbolic actions, a meal of friendship, and festive celebration.[9]

Eucharistic catechesis, which is mentioned in no. 12, should go beyond such human values. Thus, depending on their age, psychological condition, and social situation, children may gradually open their minds to the perception of Christian values and the celebration of the mystery of Christ.[10]

10.   The Christian family has the greatest role in teaching these Christian and human values.[11] Thus Christian education, provided by parents and other educators, should be strongly encouraged in relation to liturgical formation of children as well.

By reason of the responsibility freely accepted at the baptism of their children, parents are bound in conscience to teach them gradually to pray. This they do by praying with them each day and by introducing them to prayers said privately.[12] If children are prepared in this way, even from their early years, and do take part in the Mass with their family when they wish, they will easily begin to sing and to pray in the liturgical community, indeed they will have some kind of foretaste of the eucharistic mystery.

If the parents are weak in faith but still wish their children to receive Christian formation, at least they should be urged to share the human values mentioned above with their children. On occasion, they should be encouraged to participate in meetings of parents and in non-eucharistic celebrations with their children.

11.   The Christian communities to which the individual families belong or in which the children live also have a responsibility toward children baptized in the Church. By giving witness to the Gospel, living fraternal charity, actively celebrating the mysteries of Christ, the Christian community is the best school of Christian and liturgical formation for the children who live in it.

Within the Christian community, godparents and others with special concern who are moved by apostolic zeal can help greatly in the necessary catechesis of children of families which are unable to fulfill their own responsibility in Christian education.

In particular these ends can be served by preschool programs, Catholic schools, and various kinds of classes for children.

12.   Even in the case of children, the liturgy itself always exerts its own proper didactic force.[13] Yet within programs of catechetical, scholastic, and parochial formation, the necessary importance should be given to catechesis on the Mass.[14] This catechesis should be directed to the child's active, conscious, and authentic participation.[15] "Clearly accommodated to the age and mentality of the children, it should attempt, through the principal rites and prayers, to convey the meaning of the Mass, including a participation in the whole life of the Church."[16] This is especially true of the text of the eucharistic prayer and of the acclamations with which the children take part in this prayer.

Special mention should be made of the catechesis through which children are prepared for first communion. Not only should they learn the truths of faith concerning the eucharist, but they should also understand how from first communion on—prepared by penance according to their need and fully initiated into the body of Christ—they may actively participate in the eucharist with the people of God and have their place at the Lord's table and in the community of the brethren.

13.   Various kinds of celebrations may also play a major role in the liturgical formation of children and in their preparation for the Church's liturgical life. By the very fact of celebration children easily come to appreciate some liturgical elements, for example, greetings, silence, and common praise (especially when this is sung in common). Such celebrations, however, should avoid having too didactic a character.

14.   Depending on the capacity of the children, the word of God should have a greater and greater place in these celebrations. In fact, as the spiritual capacity of children develops, celebrations of the word of God in the strict sense should be held frequently, especially during Advent and Lent.[17] These will help greatly to develop in the children an appreciation of the word of God.

15.   Over and above what has been said already, all liturgical and eucharistic formation should be directed toward a greater and greater response to the Gospel in the daily life of the children.

CHAPTER II

Masses with Adults in Which Children Also Participate

16.   Parish Masses are celebrated in many places, especially on Sunday and holydays, with a large number of adults and a smaller number of children. On such occasions the witness of adult believers can have a great effect upon the children. Adults can also benefit spiritually from

experiencing the part which the children have within the Christian community. If children take part in these Masses together with their parents and other members of their family, this should be of great help to the Christian spirit of families.

Infants who as yet are unable or unwilling to take part in the Mass may be brought in at the end of Mass to be blessed together with the rest of the community. This may be done, for example, if parish helpers have been taking care of them in a separate area.

17.   Nevertheless, in Masses of this kind it is necessary to take great care that the children do not feel neglected because of their inability to participate or to understand what happens and what is proclaimed in the celebration. Some account should be taken of their presence, for example, by speaking to them directly in the introductory comments (as at the beginning and the end of Mass) and in part of the homily.

Sometimes, moreover, it will perhaps be appropriate, if the physical arrangements and the circumstances of the community permit, to celebrate the liturgy of the word, including a homily, with the children in a separate area that is not too far removed. Then, before the eucharistic liturgy begins, the children are led to the place where the adults have meanwhile been celebrating their own liturgy of the word.

18.   It may also be very helpful to give some tasks to the children. They may, for example, bring forward the gifts or sing one or other of the parts of Mass.

19.   Sometimes, if the number of children is large, it may be suitable to plan the Masses so that they correspond better to the needs of the children. In this case the homily should be directed to the children but in such a way that adults may also benefit from it. In addition to the adaptations now in the Order of Mass, one or other of the special adaptations described below may be employed in a Mass celebrated with adults in which children also participate, where the bishop permits such adaptations.

CHAPTER III

Masses with Children in Which Only a Few Adults Participate

20.   In addition to the Masses in which children take part with their parents and other members of their family (which are not always possible everywhere), Masses with children in which only some adults take part are recommended, especially during the week. From the beginning of the liturgical restoration it has been clear to everyone that some adaptations are necessary in these Masses.[18]

Such adaptations, but only those of a more general kind, will be considered below (nos. 38-54).

21.   It is always necessary to keep in mind that through these eucharistic celebrations children must be led toward the celebration of Mass with adults, especially the Masses in which the Christian community comes together on Sundays.[19] Thus, apart from adaptations which are necessary because of the children's age, the result should not be entirely special rites which differ too greatly from the Order of Mass celebrated with a congregation.[20] The purpose of the various elements should always correspond with what is said in the General Instruction of the *Roman Missal* on individual points, even if at times for pastoral reasons an absolute *identity* cannot be insisted upon.

Offices and Ministries in the Celebration

22.   The principles of active and conscious participation are in a sense even more valid for Masses celebrated with children. Every effort should be made to increase this participation and to make it more intense. For this reason as many children as possible should have special parts in the celebration, for example: preparing the place and the altar (see no. 29), acting as cantor (see no. 24), singing in a choir, playing musical instruments (see no. 32), proclaiming the readings (see nos. 24 and 47), responding during the homily (see no. 48), reciting the intentions of the general intercessions, bringing the gifts to the altar, and performing similar activities in accord with the usage of various communities (see no. 34).

To encourage participation it will sometimes be helpful to have several additions, for example, the insertion of motives for giving thanks before the priest begins the dialogue of the preface.

In all this one should keep in mind that external activities will be fruitless and even harmful if they do not serve the internal participation of the children. Thus religious silence has its importance even in Masses with children (see no. 37). The children should not be allowed to forget that all the forms of participation reach their high point in eucharistic communion when the body and blood of Christ are received as spiritual nourishment.[21]

23.   It is the responsibility of the priest who celebrates with children to make the celebration festive, fraternal, meditative.[22] Even more than in Masses with adults, the priest should try to bring about this kind of spirit. It will depend upon his personal preparation and his manner of acting and speaking with others.

Above all, the priest should be concerned about the dignity, clarity, and simplicity of his actions and gestures. In speaking to the children he should express himself so that he will be easily understood, while avoiding any childish style of speech.

The free use of introductory comments[23] will lead children to a genuine liturgical participation, but these explanations should not be merely didactic.

It will help in reaching the hearts of the children if the priest sometimes uses his own words when he gives invitations, for example, at the penitential rite, the prayer over the gifts, the Lord's Prayer, the sign of peace, and communion.

24.   Since the eucharist is always the action of the entire Church community, the participation of at least some adults is desirable. These should be present not as monitors but as participants, praying with the children and helping them to the extent necessary.

With the consent of the pastor or the rector of the church, one of the adults may speak to the children after the gospel, especially if the priest finds it difficult to adapt himself to the mentality of the children. In this matter the norms of the Congregation for the Clergy should be observed.

The diversity of ministries should also be encouraged in Masses with children so that the Mass may be evidently the celebration of a community.[24] For example, readers and cantors, whether children or adults, should be employed. In this way variety will keep the children from becoming tired because of the sameness of voices.

Place and Time of Celebration

25.   The primary place for the eucharistic celebration for children is the church. Within the church, however, a space should be carefully chosen, if available, which will be suited to the number of participants. It should be a place where the children can conduct themselves freely according to the demands of a living liturgy that is suited to their age.

If the church does not satisfy these demands, it will sometimes be suitable to celebrate the eucharist with children outside a sacred place. Then the place chosen should be appropriate and worthy.[25]

26.   The time of day chosen for Masses with children should correspond with the circumstances of their lives so that they may be most open to hearing the word of God and to celebrating the eucharist.

27.   Weekday Mass in which children participate can certainly be celebrated with greater effect and less danger of weariness if it does not take place every day (for example, in boarding schools). Moreover, preparation can be more careful if there is a longer interval between celebrations.

Sometimes it is preferable to have common prayer to which the children may contribute spontaneously, either a common meditation or a celebration of the word of God. These celebrations continue the eucharist and lead to deeper participation in later eucharistic celebrations.

28.   When the number of children who celebrate the eucharist together is very great, attentive and conscious participation becomes more difficult. Therefore, if possible, several groups should be formed; these should not be set up rigidly according to age but with regard to the progress of religious formation and catechetical preparation of the children.

During the week such groups may be invited to the sacrifice of the Mass on different days.

Preparation for the Celebration

29. Each eucharistic celebration with children should be carefully prepared beforehand, especially with regard to prayers, songs, readings, and intentions of the general intercessions. This should be done in discussion with the adults and with the children who will have a special ministry in these Masses. If possible, some of the children should take part in preparing and ornamenting the place of celebration and preparing the chalice with the paten and the cruets. Over and above the appropriate internal participation, such activity will help to develop the spirit of community celebration.

Singing and Music

30. Singing is of great importance in all celebrations, but it is to be especially encouraged in every way for Masses celebrated with children, in view of their special affinity for music.[26] The culture of various groups and the capabilities of the children present should be taken into account.

If possible the acclamations should be sung by the children rather than recited, especially the acclamations which are a part of the eucharistic prayer.

31. To facilitate the children's participation in singing the Gloria, profession of faith, Sanctus, and Agnus Dei, it is permissible to use music set to appropriate vernacular texts, accepted by the competent authority, even if these do not agree completely with the liturgical texts.[27]

32. The use of "musical instruments may be of great help" in Masses with children, especially if they are played by the children themselves.[28] The playing of instruments will help to support the singing or to encourage the reflection of the children; sometimes by themselves instruments express festive joy and the praise of God.

Care should always be taken, however, that the music does not prevail over the singing or become a distraction rather than a help to the children. Music should correspond to the purpose which is attached to the different periods for which it is introduced into the Mass.

With these precautions and with special and necessary concern, music that is technically produced may be also used in Masses with children, in accord with norms established by the conferences of bishops.

Gestures and Actions

33. The development of gestures, postures, and actions is very important for Masses with children in view of the nature of the liturgy as an activity of the entire man and in view of the psychology of children. This should be done in harmony with the age and local usage. Much depends not only on the actions of the priest,[29] but also on the manner in which the children conduct themselves as a community.

If a conference of bishops, in accord with the norm of the General Instruction of the *Roman Missal*,[30] adapts the actions of the Mass to the mentality of the people, it should give consideration to the special condition of children or should determine such adaptations for children only.

34.   Among the actions which are considered under this heading, processions deserve special mention as do other activities which involve physical participation.

The processional entrance of the children with the priest may help them to experience a sense of the communion that is thus constituted.[31] The participation of at least some children in the procession with the book of gospels makes clear the presence of Christ who announces his word to the people. The procession of children with the chalice and the gifts expresses clearly the value and meaning of the preparation of gifts. The communion procession, if properly arranged, helps greatly to develop the piety of the children.

Visual Elements

35.   The liturgy of the Mass contains many visual elements, and these should be given great prominence with children. This is especially true of the particular visual elements in the course of the liturgical year, for example, the veneration of the cross, the Easter candle, the lights on the feast of the Presentation of the Lord, and the variety of colors and liturgical ornaments.

In addition to the visual elements that belong to the celebration and to the place of celebration, it is appropriate to introduce other elements which will permit children to perceive visually the great deeds of God in creation and redemption and thus support their prayer. The liturgy should never appear as something dry and merely intellectual.

36.   For the same reason the use of pictures prepared by the children themselves may be useful, for example, to illustrate a homily, to give a visual dimension to the intentions of the general intercessions, or to inspire reflection.

Silence

37.   Even in Masses with children "silence should be observed at the proper time as a part of the celebration"[32] lest too great a role be given to external action. In their own way children are genuinely capable of reflection. They need, however, a kind of introduction so that they will learn how to reflect within themselves, meditate briefly, or praise God and pray to him in their hearts[33] for example after the homily or after communion.[34]

Besides this, with even greater care than in Masses with adults, the liturgical texts should be spoken intelligibly and unhurriedly, with the necessary pauses.

The Parts of the Mass

38.   The general structure of the Mass, which "in some sense consists of two parts, namely, the liturgy of the word and the liturgy of the eucharist," should always be maintained as should some rites to open and conclude the celebration.[35] Within individual parts of the celebration the adaptations which follow seem necessary if children are truly to experience, in their own way and according to the psychological patterns of childhood, "the mystery of faith . . . by means of rites and prayers."[36]

39.   Some rites and texts should never be adapted for children lest the difference between Masses with children and the Masses with adults become too great.[37] These are "the acclamations and the responses of the faithful to the greetings of the priest,"[38] the Lord's Prayer, and the trinitarian formula at the end of the blessing with which the priest concludes the Mass. It is urged, moreover, that children should become accustomed to the Nicene Creed little by little, while the use of the Apostles' Creed mentioned in no. 49 is permitted.

a) *Introductory Rite*

40.   The introductory rite of Mass has the purpose "that the faithful, assembling in unity, should constitute a communion and should prepare themselves properly for hearing the word of God and celebrating the eucharist worthily."[39] Therefore every effort should be made to create this disposition in the children and to avoid any excess of rites in this part of Mass.

It is sometimes proper to omit one or other element of the introductory rite or perhaps to enlarge one of the elements. There should always be at least some introductory element, which is completed by the opening prayer or collect. In choosing individual elements one should be careful that each one be used at times and that none be entirely neglected.

b) *Reading and Explanation of the Word of God*

41.   Since readings taken from holy scripture constitute "the principal part of the liturgy of the word,"[40] biblical reading should never be omitted even in Masses celebrated with children.

42.   With regard to the number of readings on Sundays and feast days, the decrees of the conferences of bishops should be observed. If three or even two readings on Sundays or weekdays can be understood by children only with difficulty, it is permissible to read two or only one of them, but the reading of the gospel should never be omitted.

43.   If all the readings assigned to the day seem to be unsuited to the capacity of the children, it is permissible to choose readings or a reading either from the *Lectionary for Mass* or directly from the Bible, taking into account the liturgical seasons. It is urged, moreover, that the individual

conferences of bishops prepare lectionaries for Masses with children.

If because of the limited capabilities of the children it seems necessary to omit one or other verse of a biblical reading, this should be done cautiously and in such a way "that the meaning of the texts or the sense and, as it were, style of the scriptures are not mutilated."[41]

44.   In the choice of readings the criterion to be followed is the quality rather than the quantity of the texts from the scriptures. In itself a shorter reading is not always more suited to children than a lengthy reading. Everything depends upon the spiritual advantage which the reading can offer to children.

45.   In the biblical texts "God speaks to his people . . . and Christ himself is present through his word in the assembly of the faithful."[42] Paraphrases of scripture should therefore be avoided. On the other hand, the use of translations which may already exist for the catechesis of children and which are accepted by the competent authority is recommended.

46.   Verses of psalms, carefully selected in accord with the understanding of children, or singing in the form of psalmody or the alleluia with a simple verse should be sung between the readings. The children should always have a part in this singing, but sometimes a reflective silence may be substituted for the singing.

If only a single reading is chosen, there may be singing after the homily.

47.   All the elements which will help to understand the readings should be given great consideration so that the children may make the biblical readings their own and may come more and more to appreciate the value of God's word.

Among these elements are the introductory comments which may precede the readings[43] and help the children to listen better and more fruitfully, either by explaining the context or by introducing the text itself. In interpreting and illustrating the readings from the scriptures in the Mass on a saint's day, an account of the life of the saint may be given not only in the homily but even before the readings in the form of a commentary.

Where the text of the readings suggest, it may be helpful to have the children read it with parts distributed among them, as is provided for the reading of the Lord's Passion during Holy Week.

48.   The homily in which the word of God is unfolded should be given great prominence in all Masses with children. Sometimes the homily intended for children should become a dialogue with them, unless it is preferred that they should listen in silence.

49.   If the profession of faith occurs at the end of the liturgy of the word, the Apostles' Creed may be used with children, especially because it is part of their catechetical formation.

c) *Presidential Prayers*

50.   The priest is permitted to choose from the *Roman Missal* texts of presidential prayers more suited to children, keeping in mind the liturgical season, so that he may truly associate the children with himself.

51.   Sometimes this principle of selection is insufficient if the children are to consider the prayers as the expression of their own lives and their own religious experience, since the prayers were composed for adult Christians.[44] In this case the text of prayers of the *Roman Missal* may be adapted to the needs of children, but this should be done in such a way that, preserving the purpose of the prayer and to some extent its substance as well, the priest avoids anything that is foreign to the literary genre of a presidential prayer, such as moral exhortations or a childish manner of speech.

52.   The eucharistic prayer is of the greatest importance in the eucharist celebrated with children because it is the high point of the entire celebration.[45] Much depends upon the manner in which the priest proclaims this prayer[46] and in which the children take part by listening and making their acclamations.

   The disposition of mind required for this central part of the celebration, the calm and reverence with which everything is done, should make the children as attentive as possible. They should be attentive to the real presence of Christ on the altar under the species of bread and wine, to his offering, to the thanksgiving through him and with him and in him, and to the offering of the Church which is made during the prayer and by which the faithful offer themselves and their lives with Christ to the eternal Father in the Holy Spirit.

   For the present, the four eucharistic prayers approved by the supreme authority for Masses with adults are to be employed and kept in liturgical use until the Apostolic See makes other provision for Masses with children.

d) *Rites before Communion*

53.   At the end of the eucharistic prayer, the Lord's Prayer, the breaking of bread, and the invitation to communion should always follow.[47] These elements have the principal significance in the structure of this part of the Mass.

e) *Communion and the Following Rites*

54.   Everything should be done so that the children who are properly disposed and who have already been admitted to the eucharist may go to the holy table calmly and with recollection, so that they may take part fully in the eucharistic mystery. If possible there should be singing, accommodated to the understanding of children, during the communion procession.[48]

   The invitation which precedes the final blessing[49] is important in Masses with children. Before they are dismissed they need some repetition and application of what they heard, but this should be done in a very few words. In particular, this is the appropriate time to express the connection between the liturgy and life.

At least sometimes, depending on the liturgical seasons and the different circumstances in the life of the children, the priest should use the richer forms of blessing but he should always retain the trinitarian formula with the sign of the cross at the end.[50]

* * * * * * *

55.　　The contents of the directory are intended to help children quickly and joyfully to encounter Christ together in the eucharistic celebration and to stand in the presence of the Father with him.[51] If they are formed by conscious and active participation in the eucharistic sacrifice and meal, they should learn day to day, at home and away from home, to proclaim Christ to others among their family and among their peers, by living the "faith, which expresses itself through love" (Galatians 5:6).

This directory was prepared by the Congregation for Divine Worship. On October 22, 1973, the Supreme Pontiff, Paul VI, approved and confirmed it and ordered that it be made public.

From the office of the Congregation for Divine Worship, November 1, 1973, the solemnity of All Saints.

By special mandate of the Supreme Pontiff.

> Jean Card. Villot
> Secretary of State
> 　　+H. Bugnini
> 　　Titular Archbishop of Diocletiana
> 　　Secretary of the Congregation for Divine Worship

NOTES

1. See Congregation for the Clergy, *Directorium Catechisticum Generale* [=DCG], no. 5: *AAS,* 64 (1972) 101-102.
2. See Vatican Council II, Constitution on the Liturgy, *Sacrosanctum Concilium* [=L], no. 33.
3. See DCG 78: *AAS,* 64 (1972) 146-147.
4. See L 38; also Congregation for Divine Worship, instruction *Actio pastoralis,* May 15, 1969: *AAS,* 61 (1969) 806-811.
5. First Synod of Bishops, Liturgy: *Notitiae,* 3 (1967) 368.
6. See below, nos. 19, 32, 33.
7. See Order of Mass with children who are deaf-mutes for German-speaking countries, confirmed June 26, 1970, by this congregation (prot. no. 1546/70).
8. See L 14, 19.
9. See DCG 25: *AAS,* 64 (1972) 114.
10. See Vatican Council II, Declaration on Christian Education, *Gravissimum educationis,* no. 2.
11. See *Ibid.,* 3.
12. See DCG 78: *AAS,* 64 (1972) 147.
13. See L 33.
14. See Congregation of Rites, instruction *Eucharisticum mysterium* [= EM], May 25, 1967, no. 14: *AAS,* 59 (1967) 550.
15. See DCG 25: *AAS,* 64 (1972) 114.
16. See EM 14: *AAS,* 59 (1967) 550; also DCG 57: *AAS,* 64 (1972) 131.
17. See L 35, 4.
18. See above, no. 3.
19. See L 42, 106.
20. See first Synod of Bishops, Liturgy: *Notitiae,* 3 (1967) 368.
21. See General Instruction of the Roman Missal [=IG], no. 56.
22. See below, no. 37.
23. See IG 11.
24. See L 28.
25. See IG 253.
26. See IG 19.
27. See Congregation of Rites, instruction *Musicam sacram,* March 5, 1967, no. 55: *AAS,* 59 (1967) 316.
28. *Ibid.,* 62: *AAS,* 59 (1967) 318.
29. See above, no. 23.
30. See IG 21.
31. See IG 24.
32. See IG 23.
33. See instruction *Eucharisticum mysterium,* no. 38: *AAS,* 59 (1967) 562.
34. See IG 23.
35. See IG 8.

36. See L 48.
37. See above, no. 21.
38. IG 15.
39. IG 24.
40. IG 38.
41. See *Lectionary for Mass,* introduction, no. 7d.
42. IG 33.
43. See IG 11.
44. See Consilium for the Implementation of the Constitution on the Liturgy, Instruction on Translation of Liturgical Texts, January 25, 1969, no. 20: *Notitiae,* 5 (1969) 7.
45. See IG 54.
46. See above, nos. 23, 37.
47. See above, no. 23.
48. See instruction *Musicam sacram,* no. 32: *AAS,* 59 (1967) 309.
49. See IG 11.
50. See above, no. 39.
51. See Eucharistic Prayer II.